The Complete Best Man

The
Complete Best Man

John Bowden

howtobooks

for Paula, my bride and joy!

Every effort has been made to identify and acknowledge the sources of the material
quoted throughout this book. The author and publishers apologise for any errors or
omissions, and would be grateful to be notified of any corrections that should appear in
any reprint or new edition.

Published by How To Books Ltd,
3 Newtec Place, Magdalen Road,
Oxford OX4 1RE. United Kingdom.
Tel: (01865) 793806. Fax: (01865) 248780.
email: info@howtobooks.co.uk
www.howtobooks.co.uk

British Library Cataloguing in Publication Data
A catalogue record for this book is available from the British Library

Cover design by Baseline Arts Ltd, Oxford
Cartoons © Colin Shelbourn www.shelbourn.com
Produced for How To Books by Deer Park Productions, Tavistock
Typeset by PDQ Typesetting, Stoke-on-Trent, Staffs.
Printed and bound by Cromwell Press, Trowbridge, Wiltshire

NOTE: The material contained in this book is set out in good faith for general guidance
and no liability can be accepted for loss or expense incurred as a result of relying in
particular circumstances on statements made in this book. The laws and regulations are
complex and liable to change, and readers should check the current position with the
relevant authorities before making personal arrangements.

Contents

Preface

Welcome, sir ... or madam. Yes, the role of best man is no longer exclusively a male preserve ... and sometimes more than one person does the job. But to have called this book *The Complete Best Man, Best Girl, Best Man and Girl and Best Men* would have been a bit of a mouthful.

In the pages that follow I talk to and about the *Best Man* and refer to that person as *he* or *him*. This stems from my desire to avoid ugly, cumbersome English (*he, she or they ... him, her or them*) and to avoid the destruction of another Amazonian rainforest. But really the book is written for *anyone* asked to do the business.

Almost everything written applies to both genders. The only exceptions are attire, where a best girl should match what the bride is wearing, but not outshine her, and a best girl's possibly different ideas as to what constitutes a brilliant stag do. If in doubt, ask the groom what he has in mind or delegate this one function to a mere male.

The book is in two parts. Part One tells you everything you need to become an impressive, efficient and effective modern best man. In Part Two you'll find out how to prepare and present a unique and memorable speech that will sparkle like vintage champagne.

While the basic responsibilities of a best man have remained largely unchanged over the years, the world has moved on. The key is to respect traditions of the past but also to keep up with the times. Unorthodox interpretations of your role are no longer a breach of social etiquette.

Similarly, while your speech should include a few time-honoured crowd-pleasers which people will expect to hear, there remains plenty of scope to stamp your own personality on it as you drag it screaming into the twenty-first century.

I've been there, done it and got the T-shirt – well several T-shirts actually. Not only that, I've written loads of other books on weddings and speechmaking. Let's make a deal. I'll give you all the advice, tips and strategies you'll need to do a fantastic job. In return, all I ask from you is your time, your mind and your commitment.

It's a serious business being a best man. There's a lot to do, a lot to remember and a lot to say. You owe it to the bride and groom – and to *yourself* – to give it your best shot. With this handbook at your side you can become the complete best man.

John Bowden

PART ONE

THE BEST MAN'S DUTIES

The Appointment

Your mobile rings:

'Hi. It's me. Fancy a pint tonight?'
'Yeah. Down the pub with the lads?'
'No. Thought we'd have a quiet drink by ourselves … I've got something to ask you …'

Words like Man and Best immediately spring into your mind. And, of course, you are right.

Your mate got engaged last week and you were half expecting this call. But unless you've already carefully thought things through, you'd be wise to lose your signal for a while. You need some serious thinking time.

Being a best man is not rocket science. But it does require a real commitment. Before we get into the pros and cons – that's fors and againsts, not tarts and baddies – of saying 'I do' to your amigo, let's have a little history lesson.

When your great-great-(and about another 50 greats)-grandfather decided to take a wife, he meant it literally … and usually from the next village. It was a case of the other man's grass is always greener … and his totty is always hotter. So over the hill the horny hun would hike – weapon in hand – to sweep a young maiden off her feet. Problem was, the menfolk of the female's family had other ideas and would give the young upstart a kick in the nuts and send him packing.

Your beloved ancestor soon got fed up of applying ice packs every Sunday morning, and decided it would be more sensible to go in mob-handed. He'd pal up with the baddest brother in his village and then invite him to be the chief henchman on his next amorous quest. This time it was the lass's brethren who got a good kicking as your great-great-(and about another 50 greats)-grandmother eventually got picked up. The old chap had indeed chosen the *best man* for the job … and without him, you wouldn't be around today. I didn't realise family history could be so much fun. Here endeth today's lesson.

Nowadays the best man's support is more moral and emotional than physical. His intention is to toast the bride, not roast her father … to slay the in-laws with rapier wit, not his rapier. With more refined duties, however, come greater responsibility. And with greater responsibility comes far more opportunities to cock it up.

Which of these is you?

> **Best Man 1**
> *'Have you got anything for a stag do for 15 guys next week in Bristol? You haven't? How about Cardiff? You're fully booked up everywhere? Thanks anyway.'*

> **Best Man 2**
> *'I'm the best man and I'm going to book a great stag do well in advance. I am organised, reliable and keen to make it the very best experience for the groom-to-be.'*

One guess which one I'd want to do the business for me. Best Man 1 is really Worst Man 1. No one is expecting a Mr Perfect, but the bottom line is that you shouldn't accept the role unless you are going to give it your best shot. And your bosom buddy must think your best shot is good enough or he wouldn't have chosen you, would he?

MAKE YOUR MIND UP TIME

Let's face it, unless you are browsing in WH Smith (other bookshops and internet suppliers are also available), the odds are you have already decided to say 'Yes', or you'd hardly be reading this literary masterpiece. If you're still not sure though, sleep on it. But don't leave it too long to decide. It would be rather embarrassing if you were to accept next Wednesday, when someone else had been given the job on Tuesday.

Had a good night's sleep? Good. And you're going to do it? Great. Your signal has been mysteriously restored … phone your mate back and agree to that drink. You need to convince him – and everyone else concerned – that you are 100% committed to being the best best man you can be. They can't ask for more than that. Thank him for choosing you (assuming the something he wanted to ask you wasn't to borrow your wheelbarrow). Congratulate him on finding such a fantastic woman. Remind him that you are available to help them both with the wedding preparations in any way they want.

Suggest the three of you get together soon to get an idea of what sort of wedding they're planning and to discuss your role in the months to come.

MEET THE EXTENDED FAMILY

Traditionally, your next job would have been to meet the four parents. But the world has changed. The nuclear family of mum, dad and two or three kids no longer exists, if it ever did. Today, families often come with a mum, dad, step-mum, step-dad, siblings, step-siblings, and even step-step siblings … family trees often have more branches than the NatWest. And at the same time an ever-increasing number of these extended families are scattering themselves all over the country – and often all over the world.

Given these sociological and demographic trends (that was the social science bit), it is hardly surprising that for a twenty-first century best man it can be a nightmare to know who (and sometimes how) to contact, and possibly who not to. What is the pecking order when it comes to seating arrangements, etiquette and all that? Get it wrong and you will cause a diplomatic fallout that will make the Middle East look like a picnic. If you are in any doubt, you simply must ask the bride and groom.

Try to meet (or at least phone) the parents/guardians/persons nominated as the main players by the happy couple. Give them plenty of positive messages and vibes. It's a bit like going to a job interview. What qualities and abilities are they looking for? Be prepared to give at least one example of a time when you have been:

➤ Cool under pressure
➤ A great organiser
➤ A model of common sense
➤ An effective communicator
➤ Punctual
➤ Responsible
➤ Thoughtful
➤ Tactful
➤ Presentable
➤ Sober(ish)

Well done, young man. On behalf of both families, I hereby declare that you *are* the best man for the job.

Now prove me right.

Countdown to the Big Day

Do you want the good news or the bad news? I can't hear you. Well, I'll tell you anyway. The good news is that officially you won't be involved with many of the wedding preparations (hooray) ... the bad news is that unofficially you will be (boo). And possibly big time. It's up to the groom and his wife-to-be to decide how much of the admin and organisational work they want to delegate to you, and to others. But you simply must find out what is expected of you ... and find out quickly. There is a trend nowadays for everyone to muck in to get things done. That's fine so long as every job gets covered ... and is not duplicated. Twelve drummers drumming, eleven pipers piping and five golden rings might be considered a little excessive.

There are loads of arrangements to be made, rituals to be observed and courtesies to be extended. This all requires planning of military precision. After all, failing to plan is planning to fail. Suggest that early meeting with the happy couple (and the chief bridesmaid, if there is one) to find out precisely who'll be doing what. Take this handbook with you, order a few bevvies, find a nice quiet table in the corner and work your way through this chapter and the detailed checklists. Every task should be allocated to a nominated individual ... or, better still, to a volunteer. By the end of the evening everyone knows *precisely* what they will be doing over the next few months and, equally importantly, what they will *not* be doing.

Before we start to think about all this organisational stuff, there are a few preliminary questions that need to be asked ... and answered.

Where and when?

It's kind of important to find out where and when the ceremony will take place. Usually it'll be in a church or registry office, but it could be on a bouncy castle or at the bottom of the sea. You need to find out precisely where and when, so that you can order your snorkel in plenty of time. Similarly, ask where the conception – sorry, reception will take place. Will the nuptials and reception take place in formal attire at Brighton's Royal Pavilion? Or will it be a quick 'I do' on Brighton Pier in Kiss Me Quick hats, followed by a slap-up fish 'n' chips in the local chippie? (Weddings really do take place at both these places – honestly.)

How many?

Put a little gentle pressure on the happy couple to decide approximately how many punters will be invited. This figure can be firmed up later (I wish mine could be), but at least a ballpark figure will give you some idea of the scale of things to come and will help you decide how many ushers will be required (usually one per 20 odd guests – or 25 normal ones).

Traditionally, formal invitations will be sent from the bride's home about six weeks before the big match takes place. You will need to RSVP along the lines:

> Ben Nevis accepts with pleasure George and Rose Bush's invitation to the marriage of their daughter, Ginger Bush, to Sydney Harbour, at … , on … , at … , and afterwards at …

Who's paying?

Mercenary, I know, but with an average wedding costing seventeen grand plus today, everyone must be absolutely clear on who's going to be picking up the various tabs. Agree this at an early stage with all the main players. You won't be expected to pay a lot towards the total bill, but you *may* need to budget for:

▶ Your own formal wear and accessories
▶ The cost of your travel and hotel bills
▶ The cost of your travel, accommodation and activities at the stag do (and maybe a contribution towards the groom's costs, so he can go free)
▶ A gift for the happy couple

Put a few extra pennies in your piggy bank each month during the engagement period. Believe me, the money will be spent. If it isn't, you won't need to live on Pot Noodles while the happy couple are enjoying champagne and caviar in the Cayman Islands.

Now we'll get down to the nitty-gritty.

CLOTHING

The bride will probably have strong views about this, and you would be wise to find out what they are. Perhaps male attendants will be asked to wear matching ties, cravats, shirts or waistcoats. Don't all dress identically, head to toe, with the groom fronting in a heavily sequinned open shirt … unless you want to look like a Smokey Robinson tribute band.

If everyone is expected to hire formal attire, this should be paid for from central funds. It's best for all the lads to get fitted on the same day. The important thing is that everyone dresses with the same degree of formality (or perhaps lack of it). For the best man, a good rule of thumb is to follow suit with the groom, but not to outshine him.

Will there be buttonholes? What flowers will be chosen and what colour(s) will they be? You may think all this to be unimportant. Believe me, it isn't. Don't spoil the bride's big day. She would not appreciate a raid by the Fashion Police. If she wants people to dress to impress, that's the way it's got to be. And that applies to everyone … including those normally allergic to soap and water.

TRANSPORT

While the groom is usually in overall charge of travel arrangements for the day, it's your job to get him to the church on time. Unless you live within walking distance of the venue, you will need to arrange some sort of transport. ('And your specialist subject?' 'The bleeding obvious.') Whether you decide to travel by taxi, three-wheeler or tandem, do a few trial runs to arrive at the same time and on the same day as you will need to when it's for real. Allow yourself a little extra time on the actual day as Sod's Law decrees traffic lights will be out of order or it will be an unannounced National Cones Day.

Will there be any official cars? It is customary to have two from the bride's home to the church and three on to the reception.

To the church
Car 1: bride and bride's dad (or whoever is giving her away)
Car 2: bride's mum (or other close relative/friend) and the main attendants

To the reception
Car 1: bride and groom
Car 2: parents (or other close relatives/friends) of bride and groom
Car 3: attendants

It is also traditional for the best man to arrange a car to take the newlyweds on the first stage of their honeymoon.

You may also be required to arrange convoys of guests from the station and later to ferry people (not necessarily in the nautical sense) to and from the reception. You need to know numbers, names and times. Bear all this in mind when selecting ushers. If they have their own wheels, then so much the better. Car hire firms can be a little unreliable. If you intend to use them, make sure you get your precise requirements agreed in writing. A verbal contract isn't worth the paper it's written on. And be warned: car hire firms can impose heavy financial penalties if vehicles are not returned/ collected by the agreed times. Consider using a minibus rather than a fleet of cars to and from the reception. It may prove more economical and at least everyone can enjoy a little bubbly.

Parking can be a nightmare. Find out where everyone can park safely and legally for the duration of the ceremony and reception. Arriving to be greeted by a 'Car Park Full' notice, an overzealous traffic warden or a brainless wheel clamper is not an auspicious start to married life.

Finally, remember Murphy's Law: If things can go wrong, they will. Be a good little boy scout and be prepared for this. Carry a list of phone numbers of local taxi firms and any other people you could rope in at short notice, should things go a little pear-shaped.

THE CEREMONY

Liaise with the clergyman or registrar
Arrange a meeting with whoever is going to officiate. Go along with

the bride and groom and discuss their hopes and wishes for the ceremony. While the officiator will do his or her best to accommodate them, there may be rules, regulations and restrictions they must comply with. Maybe confetti isn't allowed; maybe there are places where photography or videoing isn't permitted; maybe some of the traditional wedding music won't be sanctioned if the ceremony isn't in a church. Pieces like Mendelssohn's *Wedding March* and Wagner's *Bridal March* (Here Come the Bride) are often blackballed in hotels and stately homes because they are so associated with church weddings. Felix and Dickie would have found this bizarre because they composed them to be played *outside* churches (yeah, go figure).

Order of Ceremony and Wedding Day Schedule

Most couples have an Order of Ceremony sheet. This has their names (and possibly a photo) on the front together with the date and venue. It may also give the names of the supporting cast. Inside will be a list of the various stages of the ceremony together with the words of any hymns, prayers and readings. It is your responsibility to collect copies of this sheet from the bride and then pass them on to the usher charged with handing them out as people arrive.

If the couple haven't produced one already, it's a good idea to suggest that a Wedding Day Schedule is drawn up. This is for the benefit of attendants, not guests. It shows precisely what will be happening and spells out what every member of the support team should be doing at each stage. You may think this is a little OTT. But it really does concentrate minds. Collect copies at the same time as the Order of Ceremony. Keep one for yourself and distribute the others among your fellow attendants.

The House of Ushers

You have been appointed sergeant major to make sure things run like clockwork on the big day. But you can't do everything yourself … and you need someone to blame if things go wrong. So you require support from a trusty corporal (chief usher) and some privates (as it were) to help you out. These will be *your* team of helpers on the day. Traditionally ushers are unmarried brothers or other close relatives of the bride and groom … but you could slip in a ringer or two. Officially they are chosen by the groom. In practice, you need to make sure you get the right people because it will be you – not the groom – who will look a right wally if the wedding breakfast turns into a dog's dinner.

So in addition to nepotism, what factors should be considered when choosing ushers? As we have seen, it helps if they have their own transport to get people from A to B, and then on to C. Other than that, ideally they need to be more like Brad Pitt than Cec Pitt. Your designated corporal should also be capable – if you'll excuse my mixed metaphors – of coming off the bench if you were to walk under that proverbial bus … or wedding limo. Well, the show must go on. ('It's what he would have wanted.')

Ushers' responsibilities are not too onerous. At a church wedding with about 100 guests, you might have four or five helpers. The chief usher will be posted at the door to escort the bride's mother on arrival ('You're her mother? I could have sworn you were her sister.'). The second will be beside him giving out Order of Ceremony sheets as guests enter ('Lovely day for it.'). The third will stand at the foot of the aisle, doing a little gentle interrogating ('Friend or foe? … sorry, love, friend or family?', with a quick supplementary, 'Bride's or groom's guests?'). The answers to these two questions will help decide where guests are to be seated, as follows:

Left	*Right*
Bride's parents/guardians	Groom and best man
Bride's close family and bridesmaids	Groom's parents
Bride's other relatives	Groom's close family
Bride's other relatives and friends	Groom's other relatives
Bride's friends	Groom's friends
Ushers	Ushers

However, a good usher should exercise a degree of discretion. For example, any elderly or disabled guests should be asked where they would prefer to sit (barring the first two rows, unless they would have sat there anyway). If people say they are friends of both the bride and groom, they should generally be ushered to the right, as the bride tends to have more guests than the groom. Try to avoid the church tipping over by having roughly the same numbers of guests on both sides.

A fourth usher will be placed halfway down the aisle to show people to their seats ('Take a pew.'). It is a good idea for him to start packing them in from the back and then work forward. If people moan that they came early to get a good seat, he should remind them that, as the Good Book tells us, 'The first shall be last'. If there is a fifth usher, he will probably be outside in the rain directing people to the car park. (Well it's a job.)

After the ceremony, all the lads help organise transport to the reception. One of them may also be given the task of making sure that nothing or nobody gets left behind before the convoy moves on. At the reception each usher should be encouraged to mingle with the other guests and to keep an eye (but not mouth) on the food and drinks situation.

The rehearsal

A day or two before the wedding, all interested parties, including the bride, groom, bridesmaids, ushers, best man and parents/guardians, gather at the ceremony site to do a quick run-through of the ceremony. The aim is to iron out any last-minute problems (and pageboys' shirts) before the whole thing goes live. Is everyone reading from the same hymn sheet? Does everyone know where and when to stand, sit, sing? Use the occasion to familiarise yourself with the place, paying particular attention to parking arrangements, potential photo opportunities … and the whereabouts of toilets. Believe me, you will be asked about all three.

It is becoming common practice for the gang to adjourn to a Rehearsal Dinner, where they may be joined by other close friends and relatives and by any other people who have travelled a light year to be there. The atmosphere should be very informal. Relax and enjoy yourself … but have a few choice words prepared just in case. If you are asked to speak, a simple but sincere toast to the happy couple is all that is required. Keep most of your ammunition dry for use at the reception.

> 'A toast to my dear friends who are each other's best friends. Your marriage tomorrow will be so much more than a ceremony…it will be a creation. May you create a wonderful world together filled with love, laughter and life. To the bride and groom.'

Yuk? Sorry, this has to be done.

THE RECEPTION

If you have any say in the matter, encourage the bride and groom to find a place quite near the scene of the chime, avoiding ones that churn out half a dozen wedding gigs each weekend. Once the venue of the reception is known, do a recce on the joint. While the bride and groom are happily discussing menus, cake, wedding flora and other domestic matters with the manager, do a little snooping. As always, check out those parking arrangements and toilets. And find out if there is somewhere they will be able to get their things together (*Carry On* humour at its finest) before they make their excuses. Changing in the loo is far from ideal, especially once the floors are flooded.

Pecking order

If people aren't told where to sit, entry into the reception is likely to resemble the first day of the January sales. To avoid the need for the intervention of a UN peacekeeping force, the bride's parents should draw up a table plan. Diplomatically suggest who should be seated near to one another (and who should be kept well apart). Make life easier for the caterers by colour-coding the backs of chairs of any guests who are veggies, who require a gluten-free meal, or who have some other special dietary requirement (you know it makes sense, Rodney).

Catering

While you are not responsible for the catering arrangements, you *are* responsible for ensuring things run smoothly at the reception. The efficiency of caterers is key to this. Find out when meals are to be served and, later, when plates and other debris will be collected. Even the most brilliant speech can be ruined if a team of chattering caterers enters stage left and exits stage right just as you're getting into the serious bit.

Speeches

Will there be a toastmaster, or will you do the honours? The traditional order of speeches is: bride's father (or guardian), groom and then you. However, it is becoming common practice nowadays for the bride to say a few words (let's hope her name isn't Catherine Tate). Other people may also want to have their twopenn'orth. If they want to, let them … but this should be arranged well in advance. The important thing is that the toastmaster (or you) knows precisely who's going to be speaking, and in what order.

Music

Ask the bride and groom what they want to do about music. Think carefully about the sort of stuff that will be played. Even if they are seriously into rock, remember that guests may be aged anything between two and 92. And to most of them three hours of solid Trash would be rubbish. Keep it balanced. Give everybody something they like … even if you hate it. (Grandma: 'They don't write music like that any more.' Grandson: 'Thank goodness.')

Do they want a live a band? Will there be background music during pre-dinner drinks? Will there be music for dancing (for want of a better word) afterwards? Do they want to hire a DJ? Do you feel confident and competent enough to audition a band or will you choose them by recommendation (and price)? Sort out the full programme, including the timing of any breaks. Whatever you do, don't pay fully in advance, or you may end up on the day with nothing more than the sweet Sounds of Silence.

PAYMENTS

Most of this will be taken care of in advance, probably by the groom or the bride's (now) poor old dad. But carry a little cash and some plastic with you on the day in case there are some unforeseen last-minute payments to be made. A punch on the nose by an untipped cabbie may cause offence.

YOUR GIFT

With all this going on it's all too easy to forget about getting that wedding pressie and card. Your choice will be largely determined by your personal budget, but try to get something that will be a happy memento for years to come. The shareholders of the Pound Shop should not benefit from your purchase. You could select something from the wedding gift list, or maybe get a pair of wine glasses or goblets. You will get extra Brownie points if you get them inscribed. Another safe bet would be a vase or a tea set … Ming, not minging.

HONEYMOON PREPARATIONS

The groom (and maybe his bride) should have sorted all this out. Make sure they remember tickets, passports, visas, driving licence, inoculations, insurance and foreign currency. Items of a more personal nature are not your concern.

WEDDING EVE

If you're going to be doing any chauffeuring tomorrow, give the car its annual clean (yes, whether it needs it or not) and make sure there's plenty of petrol in the tank. If it's going to be a taxi job, give the company a ring to make sure they haven't forgotten you. Almost there now. Run through your speech and collect any telemessages and cards from the bride. Then get your monkey suit and other paraphernalia ready before you crash out. It will save you those all-important nanoseconds in the morning.

Easier said than done, but try to get our hero to bed early too. He's bound to be a bit nervous … and so are you. Come to think of it, I'm beginning to feel a little edgy. By all means have a quiet shandy or two. But when you find yourselves discussing the meaning of life, it's time to call it a day. The Eleventh Commandment is: Thou shalt not get blathered. It just ain't worth it.

Stag Dos and Don'ts

Okay, bestie, it's time to get down to the serious business of arranging a brilliant pre-wedding bash for the groom and his mates. Ask the condemned man for his final wishes. What sort of thing has he in mind? Does he want you to arrange everything or does he want to be involved? The odds are he will delegate most, if not all, of the responsibilities to you. After all, he has other things on his mind, like getting married.

When you were nowt but a lad a best man's job was easy, as most people's idea of a good stag do was half a dozen pints, a few shorts spiked with God knows what, followed by some seriously dodgy John Travolta impersonations on the dance floor, a vindaloo and a good honk. Nowadays people expect far more than this … or perhaps as well as this.

In those days the nearest you'd be likely to get to Iceland was sitting in the car while your mum bought the frozen peas … and the nearest you'd get to Turkey was when she was serving Christmas dinner. Today stag weekends in Reykjavik and Ankara are becoming more and more popular and affordable. Other current hotspots (and coldspots) include Amsterdam, Barcelona, Budapest, Edinburgh, Dublin, Ibiza, Prague, Tallinn and Vilnius.

And the expectations of stags have changed too. Darts has given way to drag racing. Shove-halfpenny has become surfing. Cards have been converted to combat games. Today, there is a seemingly endless array of leisure activities and pursuits available to keep the lads happy, amused and out of the watering hole … well at least until after the six o'clock watershed.

So what sort of do are you going to arrange? As with many things in life, your options are largely dictated by dosh, or lack of it. Traditionally, the groom paid for everything. Today it is far more usual for each stag to pay his own share or, better still, to pay a bit extra so the groom doesn't have to cough up anything except possibly an unsavoury combination of carrots and tomatoes.

GET ORGANISED

The do needs to be properly planned, otherwise it will descend into chaos and you will end up concerned only with crowd control and damage limitation. Meet with the groom (and his wife-to-be, if he thinks it appropriate) as early as possible to talk things through. The three main areas to cover are:

▶ Invitations
▶ Date(s)
▶ Location and activities

Invitations

Who should be invited (and who should not)? Most of the names on the team sheet will probably be automatic choices. But how well would Sandy from the flower shop get on with Animal Andrews, who only got out last week? Ask yourself whether a few days together in a Big Brother House environment would be more likely to result in mirth or murder. If you do decide to invite both, it would probably be politic not to ask them to share a room. If one of your invitations is to a beer monster, give him a drinking mate with whom he can engage in synchronised stag staggering. It is also prudent to include a show pony, to provide the laughs, and a sensible lad, to help you all find the way home.

But what about brothers and fathers? A tricky one. The groom's brother should present no problem. But the bride's brother? Certain revelations and disclosures of a personal nature brought on by the groom's copious consumption of Cognac could cause considerable embarrassment all round in the cold light of day. Often the dilemma is avoided because the brother makes his excuses since he doesn't know (m)any of the other stags (phew, that was a close one). A stag do is an important rite of passage that a groom is supposed to share with peers, not parents. But what if a father is a middle-youthed Ozzy Osbourne hellraiser? If he still likes to let his hair down, even if he hasn't got any, you may decide he would be an asset.

Once the touring party has been selected and invitations accepted, make a note of everyone's mobile number and e-mail address. Set up two circular e-mail lists, one including and the other excluding the groom. In this way you can keep him informed of travel arrangements, accommodation and daytime activities, but keep him in the dark about what's likely to be going on (and coming off) when it gets dark.

Date(s)

It is best to arrange the stag do for about a month before the big day. This will give our hero plenty of time to sober up, find his trousers and get the tattoo removed by laser treatment. Try to agree on dates that most of the potential stags would find convenient. There will always be people who can't make it. One is sure to say he can't be there whatever dates are proposed … he has such important things to do and the world must revolve around him. Every group has such a character. You know the guy I'm talking about in your little gang, don't you? Yes *him*. Ultimately, the groom must decide whether the presence of one or more elusive individuals justifies changing dates and potentially causing difficulties for everyone else.

Location and activities

I'm sure you'd love to spend some quality time together in Oz, Las Vegas or the Windies. Fact is though, unless you happen to meet the Duke of Westminster down the local next week and cultivate an instant lifelong friendship over a half of Newton and Ridleys, the odds of having enough readies to do this is at best doubtful. Your choice of location and activities therefore is dependent on your budget. How much are stags able and willing to spend? Find this out asap, appoint a treasurer (Nick Leeson wannabes need not apply) and nominate someone to regularly hound the stags for the rest of their money (an Animal Andrews character would prove an ideal candidate for this pivotal role).

You need to know what your budget is. How much money are we talking about per head? As a rough guide:

- ▶ Small budget = what you would spend on a good night out on the town
- ▶ Medium budget = the cost of a weekend break in the UK
- ▶ Big budget = enough to go on a mini-break abroad

Small budget

The best small-budget stag nights are much more than drunkathons at an old farts' pub. Why not visit a casino, rock concert or footie game? If you are planning on pubbing or clubbing, find a place which is stag-do-friendly (or at least not stag-do-unfriendly). Travel in small groups, keep your voices down and avoid eye contact with local heavies. And never argue with bouncers. You may have the more powerful intellectual argument, but they are bigger than you.

Medium budget

Things are looking up. How about arranging some entertainment and activities a little further afield? You could arrange a weekend away yourself. But it is probably worth paying a little more to get it done professionally. There are loads of companies out there who will be more than willing to grab your hard-earned cash in return for channelling your testosterone into something other than the coffers of the major brewers and the local kebab shop.

Is Mr Right (and his cronies) a clubber, an adrenaline junkie, an action man, a boy racer or a gambler? Probably more than one of these, right? But at least this will get you and him thinking about the kinds of activity he would most enjoy. After all, it is *his* last real weekend of freedom. A clubber would enjoy going to clubs (aren't you glad you bought this invaluable book?). Adrenaline junkies would get high with paragliders or parachutes (and later come down to earth with paramedics). Action men get their rocks off with abseiling or paintballing. Boy racers would be driven crazy by rally driving or quad biking. And it's odds on that gamblers would enjoy a day at the races or an evening at the dogs. Make sure all the stags know precisely what's been planned so they can bring the right clothing and footwear … or a sick note.

Why not hire a private room for the evening? Then all the fun and games before the close of play on day one can take place behind closed doors and you will be far less likely to get into a ruck with the front row of the town's first fifteen. Organise a kitty so people can't conveniently disappear to the gents when it's their round. Give the do a theme: Blues Brothers, Superheroes, Cartoon Characters ... anything you like really. Don't forget to bring along some of the usual stag night accessories such as comedy breasts, ball and chain, shackles, rubber chickens, blow-up sheep and inflatable dolls. And think about ordering some cheap(ish) customised clothes for the stags to wear. I know it sounds corny (and it is), but 15 men all with 'Tom's Farewell to Freedom Tour ... Newquay 2007' and a picture of a pair of handcuffs on their T-shirts works really well and helps foster a great team spirit (God, I'm beginning to sound like a management consultant).

Big budget

If you flash the cash, the world is your lobster. The groom may already know where he wants to go. Remember, it's *his* me-time. If he doesn't, do a bit of googling. Key in 'Stag' and your chosen activity and you'll get loads of hits. Once you have narrowed them down a bit, find out if they have any special offers. Do they do customised packages? Precisely what is included (and what is not)? Where will you be flying from? Do they have a refund policy if someone drops out (hopefully not literally)? Be a pain. Get all their answers in writing. After all, you don't want your party to be featured on *Holidays from Hell*. Once you've chosen your package, check that your passport is up-to-date (did you have that haircut for a bet?) and – if you're going to somewhere really exotic – don't forget to invite me.

TRAVEL ARRANGEMENTS

The important thing is to let everyone know what the travel arrangements are well in advance, and then to stick to them.

If it's a stag night on the town, arrange to meet in a pub in the town centre. Once all the crowd has arrived, check that you have not been joined by any unwanted randoms before you move on. If it's a stag weekend somewhere else in the UK, meet at the railway or bus station bar or café. If you're going abroad, get together in the airport bar, or – if funds allow – in the business or first-class lounge. But don't get blathered … yet. Anyone who has watched *Airline* will know that drunks are not allowed anywhere near a plane. Don't get high or you won't get high.

Treat journeys to and from your destination as part of the weekend. If you are travelling by stretch limo or hired minibus, open the bubbly and play some cheesy and classy stuff that the groom was bopping to when he was about 15 or 16. Or get hold of one of those *Now That's What I call Crap!* sorry *Music!* compilations which have been churned out two or three times a year since the early 80s. If your coach has a TV, why not play a DVD to get the lads in the right mood for the festivities and frolics to follow? Here are a few offerings that all have a stag night theme: *Stag* (Kevin Dillon); *Bachelor Party* (Tom Hanks); *The Wedding Tackle* (Adrian Dunbar); *Homer's Night Out* (*The Simpsons*, Season 1); *Staggered* (Martin Clunes); *Stag Night* (*Men Behaving Badly* 6 – Neil Morrissey and Martin Clunes). No, Clunesy hasn't paid me to plug two of his DVDs.

PRANKS AND OTHER NOCTURNAL DELIGHTS

The groom could – and should – to some degree at least, have been involved in all the arrangements we've talked about so far. But now we come to the sneaky bit. No stag do is complete without the poor old groom suffering some form of personal indignity. A prank is as synonymous with a stag do as Botox is with Anne Robinson. The key is to be funny and original, but not vindictive. How far you go is up to you, bearing in mind both his personality and whether or not he is likely to shove your head up your backside. And remember: what goes on tour stays on tour.

Try to be original. Stripping him stark bollock naked and handcuffing him to a lamppost is a bit of a cliché nowadays. Getting someone to sow cress on a soaked carpet or to paint his house the colours of his least favourite team while he is away may be funny, but it is a little extreme. (Groom, please note that I did *not* suggest this, so don't be silly and put that lawyer away ... and I *love* that new exterior colour scheme.) More usual is to do something towards the end of the do that he will (later) find amusing and is not too dangerous or likely to leave any (permanent) scars. You could do worse than leave him stranded somewhere with only a thong, little black number and pair of oversized wellies for company ... or arrange a stripper who turns out to be a shemale.

Talking of strippers (what a link), I'm sure most grooms and fellow stags would appreciate the opportunity to demonstrate an artistic appreciation of the beauty of the female form. So unless you're near the Tate Gallery or my cousin Lulu's place, you will have no real alternative other than to visit a strip joint or lap-dancing club. I know you would prefer to stay in and play Scrabble, but come on, at times we all have to make sacrifices.

The Big Day

The alarm rings. You squint at the clock. Your first bowel-loosening thoughts are of a car that won't start, a lost ring … and a lost friend. God, you will become a living joke. Will your new home be in the Andes or Outer Mongolia? You rush to the loo … the 7.35 is going to be half an hour early today. As you sit (I said sit) there, you ask yourself why you ever agreed to do all this. Abseiling down the north face of the Post Office Tower would be preferable. You get up from a warm, sticky seat, paper in hand. It won't be the last time you do this today. In less time than it takes Britney Spears to get married and divorced, you will be rising from another sweat-drenched seat … this time with your speech in hand.

Get to grips, man. If you're getting a bit worked up, your mate is probably wishing he'd invested in a family-sized pack of Andrex … and on a 'Buy One, Get One Free' deal. Reflect for a moment on the wise words of Mr Kipling: 'If you can keep your head while all about you are losing theirs … it'll be a piece of cake.' Some grooms are totally relaxed about the whole thing. The other 99.9% are not. If you can convince the groom to seize the moment and actually enjoy himself, you will be hailed a hero for years to come.

BEFORE THE WEDDING

Okay, this is the big one. Knock on his door, or phone him, to make sure he's surfaced. Ten minutes later, repeat the procedure to make sure he hasn't retreated to his sack. Throughout the day it's likely that the poor lad will be displaying some or all of the classic symptoms of Pre-Nuptial Groom Disorder (PNGD): severe hand shaking, adrenaline rushes, dry-mouthed terror, nausea … and a sudden desire to join the lads on Craggey Island. Reassure him that this is quite normal. This is going to be a day to remember … and for the right reasons.

Phone a friend

Check that the chief usher has everything under control. Ask him to contact his fellow ushers to confirm none has gone awol. If there is to be a pre-marital drink, they should be reminded where and when it will take place. Remind the bride's family that you're there to give them all the last-minute support they need. Meek, mild-mannered Clark Kent will become a man of steel. Give the belle a bell to confirm you'll call round to collect the buttonholes (and the Order of Service sheets and Wedding Day Schedules, if you haven't already). Pick up any last-minute telemessages, cards, e-mails and she-mails to be read at the reception.

Trinny and Susannah

Traditionally, you are supposed to act as a fashion guru as you help the groom get dressed for his big day. In practice, you just need to tell him how wonderful he looks, get him to check his flies (kneeling in front of him could be misinterpreted if the bride's mum suddenly bursts in) and make sure there's no dog poo on his shoes. Keep the big man busy by getting him to check he has packed everything for the honeymoon. Make sure you've got all you need for the rest of the day: clothes, accessories, your speech, dosh, plastic, legal paperwork (including licence or certificate of banns) … and a crate of Valium. Double check and then treble check. Today is not an ideal time to drop a bullock.

Lord of the Rings

It's cliché time. Take care of those rings (or the ring, if the chief bridesmaid is taking care of the bride's). It may not be on the same scale as protecting Frodo against Sauron and the rest of the baddies, but lose them and you'll be as popular as the Glazer brothers at Old Trafford. Keep a substitute ring in your pocket, just in case. Anything ring-shaped and sized will do … even a Hula Hoop. If it's not needed, it can be used later to bribe any unruly pageboy or young bridesmaid. I find it generally takes more than a Hula Hoop to bribe an older bridesmaid … but you could try.

Get him to the pub on time

It is common practice nowadays for all male attendants to get together with the groom for a final pre-wedding pint of Dutch courage. It is best to choose a hostelry within walking distance (*not* staggering distance) of the venue for the ceremony. The time for gentle argument and subtle persuasion is now past. If he's still suffering from a bout of PNGD, bundle him into the back of your car and activate the childproof locks. Then frogmarch him into the pub. Once he is securely chained to his seat, phone or text the bride's dad to let him know all is well. Convention demands the injection of a little gallows humour at this stage. And come on, Mr Motivator, you've got a captive audience here. Get the lads really psyched up for the main event.

AT THE WEDDING

And so to wed. The ushers should be at their posts at least half an hour before the ceremony is due to start. You and the groom need to arrive about ten minutes later. If you are given the opportunity, pay any outstanding church or registrar fees before the service (it's a bit of an anti-climax afterwards). Get someone to take a snap of you shaking the groom's hand (or his neck, if PNGD persists) as you are about to enter the building. Turn your mobiles off and take your places in the front right pew.

The big wait

This is another stressful time for your mate. He's probably more nervous than a moggie in a room of pitbulls. Help him out. Provide his moral support. Mutter reassuring words. Keep chatting away ('Did you find Marx's vision of a post-capitalist state persuasive?', or perhaps, 'Have you heard the one about the nun and the bicycle …?'). The last guest to arrive will be the bride's mum (or guardian), who will be escorted to the inside left position by the chief usher. You will be prompted to stand shortly after the bride arrives. Glance back to make sure it's the right girl, then step forward and stand a pace behind and to the right of the groom.

The ring

Keep the ring (or rings) in your front pocket, not on your finger. You may get £250 for a camcorder calamity, but is it worth the public humiliation of the spectacle of a bride and groom tugging at the ring, while their parents are violently pulling you in the opposite direction? It is? Oh, alright then.

Signing the register

The deed is done. Now they just need a few autographs to sell on e-bay. It is usual for the bride and groom and two of the parents to provide illegible scrawls. Occasionally, however, the best man and chief bridesmaid are asked to sign on the dotted line.

The traditional order of departure from the church is:

- ▶ Bride and groom
- ▶ Bride's father (or guardian) and groom's mother (or guardian)
- ▶ Groom's father (or guardian) and bride's mother (or guardian)
- ▶ You and chief bridesmaid
- ▶ Rest of the world

While the paparazzi may have decided to give this one a miss, there are still likely to be more digital cameras, camcorders and video mobiles clicking away than on Oscars Night. So keep smiling ... and don't pick your nose or scratch your bum.

Photo opportunities

Unless the happy couple have made an exclusive deal with *OK!* or *Hello!*, it's pretty much a free-for-all when it comes to taking post-nuptial pics. This is brilliant as it gives you the chance of scrounging loads of snaps to make up a surprise wedding album while they are away enjoying sea, sun and ... sand. Professional photographers will know all the best local backdrops for their snaps (recently dug graves are not to be recommended). They will appreciate it if you can help make sure the right people are in the right shots. Otherwise for years to come everyone will be wondering about that mystery guy in the back row ('I thought he was with your family' ... 'I thought he was with yours'). Once all the traditional wedding photos are in the can, get a few informal ones. The bride lying across the arms of the groom, you and the ushers is always a favourite ... especially with horny teens.

It's time to get the show back on the road. Put on your most assertive voice and announce that the bubbly should be nicely chilled by now. Tell any stragglers that the last to arrive pays for the first round. That should speed things up. We have a convoy.

AT THE RECEPTION

The receiving line

This is an outmoded wedding day filler that deserves to be consigned to history. People wait in line as if to pay their last respects to some poor old sod lying in an open coffin. The ensuing human traffic jam makes the M25 look like an easy ride. The traditional order of handshakes and pecks on the cheek is as follows:

► Bride's mum and dad (or guardians)
► Groom's ditto
► Bride and groom

Some couples also want their best man and chief bridesmaid to be at the end of the line. If you are to be included, get the ushers to guide people to the shakeathon. If you are not, it's down to you. If the reception is less formal (or more enlightened), simply guide people towards trays of champagne (and soft drinks). No one will complain about that.

Update your speech

Take it easy on the booze and think about one or two of the more amusing or poignant moments of the day so far. Could you make a passing reference to them in your speech? That would add a bit of topicality and give the impression that all your words of wit and wisdom are spontaneous. In reality, of course, 99% of them will have been planned, rehearsed and fine tuned well in advance.

Stand and deliver

It is usual for speeches to be made *after* the guests have eaten. However, some couples prefer to have them *before* the meal, especially if some of their friends and family are known to be a little rowdy after a drink or ten. If there's no toastmaster, you will have to do a bit of MC-ing, announcing when dinner is to be served and the order of speeches. Once you are all ready to strut your stuff, stand up confidently and jingle a spoon in a wine glass to get people's attention. It's showtime.

FINAL DUTIES

The pressure's off now. It's time to relax and have some fun. Pour yourself a mug of Dom Perignon … you deserve it. Greet your adoring public. Carry a gaggle of admiring guests along the rounds to catalyse inter-table introductions and then deposit them in your wake as you move on.

If music be the food of love

The newlyweds will be first to take to the dance floor. When Robbie gets to the second chorus (you know, the contraception bit: 'She offers me protection, a lot of love and affection'), you and the chief bridesmaid should join them. Before long everyone else will be bopping away alongside you, arms waving rhythmically overhead.

When knee sliding begins, you know it's time to make your temporary excuses. Make sure all the penguin suits have been collected and hide all the pressies from that dodgy-looking geezer at the bar. The bride will have made a mental inventory and will not appreciate it if one of her five George Foremans, seven toasters, or 11 steak knife sets is half-inched to the accompaniment of *Thief in the Night*.

Okay, it's another cliché, but decorating the car is a wedding day ritual that simply must be observed. Spray 'Just Married' across the

rear windscreen, tie tin cans to the rear bumper, or attach streamers to the wing mirror and balloons to the aerial.

Remember that bridesmaid you spotted adjusting her dress five hours ago? She seems a little merry now. Open another jeroboam. This is the time to make your move …

Checklist 1
Countdown to the Big Day

This checklist gives you an idea of what – and approximately when – things need to be done. The important thing is to pre-book as much as you can, as soon as you can ... and then regularly confirm that they have not forgotten you.

12 MONTHS TO GO

✓ Discuss wedding plans with the bride and groom (and chief bridesmaid). Tactfully establish who will be paying for what.

✓ Start saving towards the stag do and any other expenses you are likely to incur (clothes, gifts, travel, hotel).

✓ Who will be doing what? Find out precisely what your role will be. Make sure all the jobs are covered ... but not duplicated.

✓ Ask the bride and groom who you should contact ... and possibly who you should not.

✓ Try to meet – or at least phone – as many of the other attendants and family members as you can.

✓ Make a note of the date of the Big Day in a diary together with the venues for the ceremony and reception.

✓ Start thinking about your speech ... it's never too soon.

✓ Try to be available as much as you can in the week before the wedding ... if possible, take a few days off work.

9 MONTHS TO GO

✓ Attend the engagement party ... if there is one.

✓ Go with the bride and groom to meet the clergyman or registrar ... discuss arrangements. Check out parking and toilets.

✓ Go with the bride and groom to the venue for the reception. Yes ... check out parking and toilets. Is there anywhere the couple can change? If necessary, confirm that the place has a licence for booze and live music.

✓ Sort out the music for the reception. Will there be a DJ? If there's going to be a band, agree the complete programme, including the timing of any breaks. Themed weddings are becoming popular ... problem is, you have to restrict yourself to the type of music linked with it. Don't pay the full fee in advance.

✓ Discuss wedding outfits with the bride and groom. Get in contact with suppliers and check the availability of clothes and accessories.

✓ Back to your speech ...

✓ Start thinking about the stag do (largely in conjunction with the groom ... but don't discuss any nocturnal add-ons).

6 MONTHS TO GO

✓ Confirm the approximate number of guests.

✓ Help the groom choose the ushers (usually one for every 20 guests). Make sure you are happy with his choice, then meet them and explain their duties.

✓ Remind the groom that he needs to arrange transport ... and possibly a photographer/videographer.

✓ Arrange transport for the groom and you to the ceremony.

✓ Arrange transport to and from the reception ... and possibly from railway stations, etc.

✓ Arrange a going-away car for the bride and groom from the reception, if required.

✓ Keep working on your speech.

4 MONTHS TO GO

✓ Discuss wedding plans with the bride and groom in greater detail.

✓ Pass these details on to other members of the wedding party.

✓ Confirm transport arrangements have been sorted.

✓ Compile a list of close family members and friends who should have special seating arrangements at the ceremony ... let the ushers know.

✓ Don't forget your speech.

✓ Choose wedding outfits together.

3 MONTHS TO GO

✓ Buy a gift and card for the wedding couple.

✓ Advise the wedding couple to produce Order of Ceremony sheets and Wedding Day Schedules.

✓ Ask the bride's parents/guardians/carers to draw up a table plan for the reception. Will there be a toastmaster, or will you do the honours?

✓ Yes ... carry on working on your speech.

✓ Confirm all the arrangements for the stag do.

6 WEEKS TO GO

✓ Formally accept your invitation to the wedding.

✓ If possible, arrange for all the male attendants to get fitted on the same day.

✓ Start putting your speech together.

4 WEEKS TO GO

✓ Ask the bride about buttonholes.

✓ Rehearse your speech. Rework it, if necessary.

✓ Enjoy the stag do.

3 WEEKS TO GO

✓ Recover from the stag do.

✓ Meet the ushers and give them duty lists. Confirm they know what they will be doing … and when they will be doing it.

✓ Check for roadworks, diversions, etc. taking place on the wedding day … revise timings as necessary.

✓ Do a trial run to the ceremony and reception venues on the same day and the same times as you will on the Big Day.

✓ Confirm with the bride and groom who will be speaking at the reception and in what order.

✓ Rehearse your speech.

✓ Confirm that the groom has the wedding ring.

1 WEEK TO GO

✓ Check the bridegroom has all the necessary documents for the wedding and honeymoon … double check passports and visas.

✓ Attend the wedding rehearsal. Sort out any last-minute problems. Confirm parking arrangements, whereabouts of toilets and best locations for photographs.

✓ Attend the rehearsal dinner – if there is one – and have a few words prepared, just in case.

✓ Liaise with the ushers on final arrangements.

✓ Collect Order of Ceremony sheets and Wedding Day Schedules from the bride. Give the Order of Ceremony sheets to the usher who will be handing them out. Give the Wedding Day Schedules to your fellow attendants. (Don't forget to keep one for yourself.)

✓ Confirm that all the travel arrangements are in place.

✓ Yes … rehearse your speech.

✓ Make another trial run to the ceremony and reception venues.

✓ Make a note of details and availability of emergency taxi companies.

✓ Buy/collect decorations for the getaway car.

✓ Give the bride and groom their gift and card.

✓ Organise decorations for the going-away car.

✓ Time for a makeover?

1 DAY TO GO

✓ Charge up your mobile.

✓ Withdraw plenty of cash.

✓ Buy something ring-shaped and sized, just in case. Put it in your wallet.

✓ Collect messages from absent friends from the bride.

✓ Check that the groom has the ring … and knows where it is.

✓ Go with the groom to collect hired clothing and accessories.

✓ Arrange the time you will arrive at the groom's place tomorrow (if you will be getting ready and leaving from there).

✓ Confirm arrangements for collecting buttonholes from the bride.

✓ Wash your car and fill it up if you are driving to the ceremony.

✓ Make sure any hired transport outfits haven't forgotten about you.

✓ Practise your speech.

✓ Put the phone numbers of (emergency) taxi firms in your wallet.

✓ Encourage the groom to have an early night.

✓ Pray.

Checklist 2
The Stag Do

If you work around the following key prompts, you won't go far wrong …

✓ Allow plenty of time to get things organised.

✓ Have the do about a month before the main event.

✓ Know the score … it's not just about you and the ushers … the main man is the groom … what sort of things does he want to do?

✓ Who will be invited … and who will *not*?

✓ Consider the lads … any special needs or health concerns? … any age or travel considerations?

✓ The bottom line. Let's talk cash… how much are we talking about here? Will stags also be paying for/contributing to the groom's costs?

✓ Location, location, location. Which factor(s) will help you choose yours … recommendation, great deal, significance to the groom, convenience, accessibility, budget, activities, style (or lack of it)?

✓ Beware of clashes … no, not stag weekend attire, but anything else important to the main players going on (footie, birthdays, anniversaries, public holidays?).

✓ Give it a theme … anything you and the groom like, really. Hire or buy a couple of 80s or 90s CDs and maybe a stag-related DVD.

✓ Think about your prank (I said prank) … something funny and original, but nothing (too) vindictive.

✓ Military precision. You may need to co-ordinate a lot of people … demand commitment from fellow stags. Keep in touch with everyone during the build-up (through e-mail, mobile, etc.). Give them a contact number.

✓ Start collecting the dosh. If you don't show them who's boss, this could prove more testing than a Russian crossword. Keep comprehensive records and keep the pressure on the lads. If necessary, appoint a suitable (big) enforcement officer.

✓ Do your homework … check out transport, activities, dress code, all necessary paperwork.

✓ Pre-book as much as you can.

✓ Don't lose it. Have fun … but look after the groom (the original purpose of a best man) … and yourself.

✓ Take photos and video clips, but later edit carefully. What goes on on tour stays on tour.

✓ Think about the morning after. Drink at least a pint of water and leave the window open before you crash out … it helps.

✓ Keep her sweet … your good lady was good enough to give you a weekend pass, so to avoid the Spanish Inquisition on your return, tell her how boring it was … and bring her a gift … and not the stripper's G-string.

Checklist 3
The Big Day

The Big Day has arrived. Keep calm and follow these guidelines ...

BEFORE THE CEREMONY
✓ Make sure the condemned man is up (as it were).

✓ Get in contact with all the other main players to ensure there are no last-minute hitches before the happy couple get hitched.

✓ Check the ushers know their duties.

✓ Get to the groom's pad at the arranged time.

✓ Make sure the groom looks his best.

✓ Reassure him ... everything will be fine.

✓ Make sure he has packed (if they are going away today) and has all the necessary paperwork.

✓ Take care of the ring(s), including the spare one ... even a Hula Hoop will do. Don't keep the spare one in the same place as the real thing(s).

✓ Take plenty of cash and plastic.

✓ Take an emergency kit for the groom, just in case. Include a comb and a handkerchief.

✓ Final run-through of your speech. Don't forget to take the script with you.

✓ Time for a final drop of Dutch courage with the lads? … and make sure it is no more than a drop.

AT THE CEREMONY

✓ Arrive about 20 minutes early … don't forget to take the groom with you.

✓ Switch your mobile off.

✓ If possible, pay any outstanding fees before the main event.

✓ Stand to the groom's right in the front right pew.

✓ Hand over the ring, when prompted.

✓ Sign the register, if required.

✓ Leave the ceremony alongside the chief bridesmaid, immediately behind the groom's father (or guardian) and the bride's mother (or guardian).

✓ Help co-ordinate the photo session.

✓ Announce that it is time to move on to the reception.

✓ Escort the bride and groom to the car.

AT THE RECEPTION

✓ Join the receiving line, if the happy couple want you to … and if they have one.

✓ Mingle and make sure everyone is offered a drink.

✓ Guide people to their seats.

✓ Make sure the music men (and women) know what and when to play.

✓ Do the MC-ing, if required.

✓ Think about something topical you can add to your speech.

✓ Deliver your speech and read messages from absent friends.

✓ Propose a toast to the happy couple.

✓ Invite the chief bridesmaid to dance and then join the bride and groom on the dance floor.

✓ Look after the pressies.

✓ Decorate the going-away car … if the bride and groom are going away today.

✓ Bag a bridesmaid (an optional extra).

FINAL DUTIES

✓ Return any hired suits and accessories.

✓ Keep an eye on the couple's place(s) while they are away.

✓ Take this book back to the library … or sell it on e-bay.

✓ Emigrate if you've cocked it up.

Checklist 4
Your Speech

You will probably need to read Part Two of the book before this checklist makes complete sense to you. However, it seems sensible to keep all these prompt sheets together, so here we go ...

ONCE YOU HAVE ACCEPTED THE ROLE
✓ Start thinking about what you could include in your speech (and what you must definitely leave out).

✓ Remember the ground rules: aim to make it funny, uplifting, inclusive, personal, relevant and original. It should include a character attack on the groom ... but it should also be a tribute to the newlyweds. It should also be short (10 minutes max).

✓ Jot down your ideas for potential material in a notebook.

✓ Make up an original, relevant (and hopefully funny) final message to read out after the genuine ones.

✓ Plan a great opening and close ... and don't forget to thank the groom on behalf of the bridesmaids at the beginning ... and make a toast at the end.

6 WEEKS TO GO
✓ Start writing your script.

✓ Think about the best structure for your speech.

✓ Select your best/most relevant material and dump the rest.

✓ Don't be offensive or (c)rude.

✓ Link the speech together logically using link words and bridge lines.

✓ Speak your speech out loud. Does it work? Rework it until it does.

✓ Rehearse, rehearse, rehearse.

THE BIG DAY

✓ Add one or two references to things that have gone on earlier in the day.

✓ Don't drink too much (before the speech, anyway).

✓ Don't put on an act … be yourself made large.

✓ Be conversational … be relaxed … be heard.

✓ Enjoy yourself.

PART TWO

YOUR SPEECH

Ground **5** Rules

I don't want to be a spoilsport, but if you are going to prepare and present a brilliant speech you must stick to the ground rules. That doesn't mean you need to change from your trendy tuxedo into a straitjacket. Far from it. This is *your* gig. It simply means you are speaking at your friends' wedding reception, not at a stag do or a funeral.

Know your purpose

Your job is to respond to the groom's toast on behalf of the bridesmaids (and other attendants), make an hilarious and uplifting speech, toast the bride and groom and rush to the bar (or loo). Not much to ask, is it? Well no, it isn't. Read on.

Make happy talk

This is a joyous day. Your speech should reflect this. It is a tribute to the happy couple. This is not a time to share your personal woes, paint a gloomy picture of the present or offer dire predictions about the future. If the crowd wanted that they could have stayed at home and watched the News.

The bride's dad and her new hubby will have probably done more than enough of the serious and emotional stuff. What the audience wants now is to sit back, listen to a few kind words about the newlyweds … and have a good laugh at the groom's expense.

Be original

Don't buy a speech. It *cannot* be original, personal and relevant, no matter what 'personalisation' sites might tell you. If you accept the role, you shouldn't treat your speech as a chore where you look for an easy way out.

Many people have donated their speeches to wedding websites. Highly laudable, I'm sure, but they are of limited value to a thinking best man. If you crib one-liners and jokes from 5-star speeches, the odds are that many in the crowd will have heard them spoken by other speakers who have cherry-picked exactly the same material. If you steal stuff from 1-star speeches, by definition you will be regurgitating garbage.

Try to be as original as you can. That does not mean you shouldn't make use of other people's material. After all, *they* probably did. What it does mean is that you shouldn't simply lift jokes or stories. I'm not arguing morality here, I'm arguing practicality … it won't work. That said, there's nothing wrong with adapting and personalising stuff you read or hear so it fits your precise requirements and becomes unrecognisable from its source. All speakers do it.

Keep your eyes and ears open. Inspiration can come at any time. Let's say our hero is the wrong side of 20 stone and he loves golf. You overhear the following down the pub:

'That man is so fat he has to look in a mirror to find out what colour socks he's got on.'

That line could work well in your speech … with a bit of adaptation and personalisation. You say:

> 'Do you know what [groom's] golf handicap is? I'll tell you. When he puts the ball down where he can reach it, he can't see it … and when he puts it where he can see it, he can't reach it.'

Now that's being creative and original.

By all means read other people's speeches, including the Sample Speeches in this book, to get a feel about style and tone, to see what works and what bombs, and to pick out a few gags you may be able to adapt and personalise. But please don't cut and paste huge blocks of text.

In the same way that a woman doesn't want to turn up in the same dress as anyone else, so the best man should take pride in not turning up with the same speech as anyone else.

Content

It's fine to be a little risqué … in fact that's expected ('I must close now … I've got a fair bit to do back at the flat'). But don't ruin the bride's big day by saying anything that undermines the institution of marriage or questions her morals. And don't model yourself on Bernard Manning or any other blue comic. If you sink to the lavatorial, your speech will be crap.

Here are some green, amber and red topics for your speech. Green means safe as houses. Amber means they could be included, in moderation, if you know the crowd is pretty broad-minded. Red means don't even think about it. As we are continually reminded, greens are good for you.

GREEN

✓ Childhood
✓ School
✓ College
✓ Jobs
✓ Hobbies
✓ Characteristics
✓ Friends

✓ Ambitions
✓ The perfect match
✓ How they met
✓ How you met
✓ The venue (positive)
✓ The food (positive)
✓ Compliments

AMBER

? The stag do (daytime)
? The honeymoon
? Admitting your nervousness

? Mother-in law jokes (if you are sure she and her partner won't be offended)

RED

✗ Exs
✗ Anything iffy about the bride
✗ Divorce
✗ Unemployment
✗ Addictions or counselling
✗ Brushes with the law (unless minor and one-off)
✗ Sexually-transmitted diseases
✗ Fetishes
✗ Knocking marriage or weddings

✗ Smutty jokes
✗ Racist, sexist or homophobic jokes
✗ The stag do (evening) – respect the Law of Stag
✗ The venue (negative)
✗ The food (negative)
✗ The bridesmaid you have the most wet dreams about

Be positively insulting

Your speech should include a humorous character assassination of the groom … but all your insults and asides must be good-natured.

Smile as you turn the knife. Think about his looks, characteristics, job, hobbies. There is bound to be plenty of scope for humour here.

It's fine to exaggerate and parody his little foibles, but your speech will only be truly effective if the audience recognises that all your gags and observations are based upon fundamental truths about him. If our golfing heavyweight has no dress sense, you could say:

> 'Doesn't [groom] look wonderful? They made great suits in the 1980s ... He told me he bought that tux for a ridiculous figure ... Looking at him today, I'm afraid I must agree.'

But there's no point in telling the most hilarious joke about his beer-drinking exploits if his mates know his idea of a heavy night on the town is two pints of lager and a packet of cheese and onion crisps.

Be inclusive

Choose your material with care. This is easy when all the group know each other – and they all know the bride and groom. At a wedding reception this is often *not* the case. People will soon lose interest if you rabbit on and on about people and places they don't know. Let's assume only half the guests know the groom is a tight-fisted so-and-so. Don't bore the others by relating a long story to illustrate the point. One simple gag will do the job:

> '[Groom's] quite well off ... but he never brags about it. In fact you could spend an entire evening with him down the pub and never know he's got a penny.'

Now *everyone* should find that amusing – with the possible exception of Mr Skinflint.

Sugar your teasing remarks with praise

You also need to offer a few optimistic thoughts about the bride, the groom and the marriage. Don't worry, you don't need to divide your speech into funny and congratulatory bits, or embarrass yourself and others by using gushing, extravagant language. A sincere compliment and a teasing jibe often fit well together, each reinforcing the other in a kind of verbal synergy. The trick is first to set up a situation which you can exploit with a teasing remark, before turning this into a genuine compliment. If the praise comes immediately after the crowd has had a good laugh, its effect on them will be at least doubled.

'When I asked [groom] about the wedding arrangements (set-up), he said, "Oh, I'll leave all that to you. But I do want Bells - and at least three cases of it (tease)." Well I don't know about Bells, but I work with [groom] at Grange Hill Comprehensive - and I can tell you he's certainly one of the best Teachers I know (praise).'

Alternatively, you can build up the bridegroom with a public compliment, before bringing him down to earth with a bang. You simply reverse your tease and praise.

'As you all know, [groom] sells widgets for a living (set-up). His boss says he is unquestionably the most independent salesman he has ever known (praise) ... he doesn't take orders from anyone (tease).'

Length

Whatever your other half may tell you to the contrary, size *does* matter. People today have the attention span of a cabbage. Eight to ten minutes of chatter is plenty long enough. Don't suffer from the illusion that you can make your speech immortal by making it everlasting. Stand up to be seen, speak up to be heard and sit down to be appreciated.

Planning Your Speech

We asked a hundred wedding guests what a best man's most important job was. Guess what they all replied? That's right. Even if you are the most efficient, courteous and charming best man in the history of the universe, you will immediately become a serious contender for Jerk of the Year if you screw up your speech. No pressure there then.

Exceptionally, a best man can jot down a few hilarious anecdotes on Wedding Eve and then ad lib with the best of them, regaling both sides of the wedding party with excitement, empathy, enthusiasm, warmth and flair. And then there's everyone else. Most of us need at least a couple of pints before we can even think about being funny – and then only with people we know are polite or silly enough to laugh at our feeble attempts at humour. The very thought of standing, soberish, in front of a sea of sequins, suits and silent stares is a chilling prospect.

The solution is simple. Don't leave it to the last minute. The earlier you start thinking about your speech the better.

A great speech – your speech – needs to be personal, relevant and original. That's why I can't provide a simple template where you insert a few names, places and dates. What I *can* do is give you a loose skeleton. It is *your* job to put the flesh on the bones.

A BASIC STRUCTURE

Get a notebook and write the following headings on every other page:

► Opening lines and response on behalf of the bridesmaids
► Introduce yourself
► Set the tone
► Make a few general compliments
► Roast the groom
► Praise the groom
► Compliment the bride
► Congratulate the happy couple
► Offer a few pearls of wisdom
► Read the messages
► Big finish and toast

Some of your best ideas are likely to come at the most unlikely times – while shopping, watching TV, going to the loo. When you think of something that could work well for you, make a note of it on the relevant page. Use your notebook to collect enough ammunition on each of the broad areas you are expected to cover. Later you can get creative by playing around with things ... perhaps changing the order, adding something new, or joining a few bits together.

But we're running ahead of ourselves. At this stage you just need to start getting some ideas down on paper. And the more time you allow yourself to do this, the better the speech is likely to be.

OPENING LINES AND RESPONSE ON BEHALF OF THE BRIDESMAIDS

Grab the crowd's attention with a killer opening line. It doesn't have to be hilarious (although it helps if it is), but try to make it funny and original. Whatever you do, don't open the chatting with an old chestnut or an internet or e-mail favourite that people have probably heard or read a dozen times before.

Here are some possibilities to give you an idea of the right style and tone. Try to devise or adapt your own.

'Ladies and Gentlemen, [groom] just asked me "Would you like to speak now, or should we let our guests enjoy themselves a little longer?"'

'Ladies and Gentlemen, what can I say about [groom] that hasn't already been said in open court?'

'Good Ladies, afternoon and Gentlemen ... I knew I should have rehearsed this speech.'

'Ladies and Gentlemen, just once in a lifetime you get the opportunity to talk about a man blessed with dynamic charisma, devastating wit, stupendous talent and unstoppable personality ... but until that day comes along, I shall talk about [groom].'

'Ladies and Gentlemen, this speech won't take long. My suit has to be back in twenty minutes.'

'Ladies and Gentlemen, I'm making this speech today under a considerable handicap - I'm sober.'

Here are some more openers suitable for a Best Girl and a Best Man double act:

'Ladies and Gentlemen, my name is [best girl] and as you can see I'm not a man. I think [bride] may have had an influence on [groom's] choice of best person. She told me she wanted a quiet, simple wedding and that's what she got. After all, I'm quiet and [groom] is ... a very nice man.'

'Ladies and Gentlemen, I'm [best girl]. Yes, I'm a girl. [Groom] wanted to break with tradition. I'm delighted he did ... but I have to tell him and you right now, I have no intention of breaking with tradition. I may be a member of the gentle sex, but this speech is going to be anything but gentle.'

'Ladies and Gentlemen, no you're not seeing double – yet. I'm [best man 1] and this is my partner in crime [best man 2]. We hope you will compare us favourably with Morecambe and Wise, Ant and Dee, and Baddiel and Skinner. But the way [best man 2] has been putting them back today, there's a danger you may remember us as Drunk and Disorderly.'

'Ladies and Gentlemen, hi, I'm [best man 1] and this is [best man 2]. Why does it take two best men to talk about [groom], I hear you ask yourselves. Well, as the man in Moss Bros said, "There's an awful lot to fit in." '

Once you've got them laughing, get the response on behalf of the bridesmaids out of the way before you forget:

'First of all, on behalf of the bridesmaids, I'd like to thank [groom] for his warm-hearted words. It's amazing what people will say when they're not under oath.'

'On behalf of all the attendants, I'd like to say thank you for those generous words. Yes, the bridesmaids did a great job in helping [bride] up the aisle today ... but [groom], you'll be relieved to know she came to the church of her own free will.'

'Thank you, [groom], for those kind words about the bridesmaids and attendants, though I would have gone even further. They are the most delightful set of bridesmaids I have ever seen. Be honest, today you are blinkered and you only have eyes for [bride] – and who can blame you?'

INTRODUCE YOURSELF

Let the punters know who you are. You could add something about how you met the groom, why he chose you, your role today ... and how you feel about this. It's also a good idea to tell a gag against yourself. Show them you don't take yourself too seriously. Self-mockery offends nobody and reminds the crowd what a likeable, loveable chap you are.

'For those of you who don't know me, I'm [best man]. I've known [groom] since we were kids. There's nothing I wouldn't do for him, and I know there's nothing he wouldn't do for me. In fact, we spend our lives doing nothing for each other.'

'When [groom] asked me to do the business for him, I told him that I was honoured, but I felt he'd be better off with someone else. Then he offered me twenty quid. I was

indignant – I'm not a man who can be bought! Then he upped
his offer to fifty … Anyway, my name is [best man] and it's
a pleasure and privilege to be [groom's] best man today.'

'I'm [best man] and I've known [groom] since our uni days.
I'm delighted he has given me the opportunity to say a few
words about him here today. It's a big honour and makes a
nice change from being his character witness in court.'

'Hi, I'm [best man]. [Groom] and I have worked together at
[name of company] for years. One of my duties as best man
was to ensure he chose his clothes wisely. There wasn't a suit
in the shop that he didn't try on. And I'm sure you'll agree,
he eventually made the right choice. What I couldn't
understand though was why he asked the shop owner to throw
in a spare pair of underpants.'

'Hello, people, I'm [best man] and [groom] and I have been
best mates since our school days. I have to tell you that in all
the years I've known him, no one has ever questioned his
intelligence. In fact, I've never heard anyone mention it. If I
ever needed a brain transplant I'd choose his … because I'd
want one that had never been used.'

'In case any of you don't know already, I'm [groom's] little
brother [your name]. I would just like to stress – especially
to the bridesmaids – that "little" refers to our age difference
… not to any physical characteristic.'

SET THE TONE

Let people know what's in store for Mr Right. Whet their appetite for the onslaught to follow.

'My job today is to talk of [groom] – and there are no skeletons in his cupboard – or so I thought …'

'I'm supposed to sing the bridegroom's praises and tell you all about his good points. Unfortunately, I can't sing … and he hasn't any good points.'

'Last night, while I sat on the couch putting this speech together, I reviewed the high points of [groom's] life … and fell asleep.'

MAKE A FEW GENERAL COMPLIMENTS

It's time for a bit of good, old-fashioned sincerity. So **welcome** the guests, **congratulate** the newlyweds, **flatter** the bridesmaids, **thank** the hosts and **praise** – well praise just about everyone and everything. Praise the hosts ('the nicest of people'), the groom ('the luckiest man in the world'), the bride ('doesn't she look radiant?'), the occasion ('this wonderful event'), the room ('these magnificent surroundings') and the meal ('it was nice to see the menu was in French – it made such a pleasant surprise each time the food arrived'). As always, try to balance genuine compliments with a few teasing remarks.

'To echo [groom's] welcoming words, thank you all for being here today. We have guests from all over the world. New South Wales, Tonga, Timbuktu … these are the only three places not represented.'

'All our congratulations go to the happy couple. May you have a wonderful life together. I don't wish to sound sexist, but there's no doubt about it, men have better taste than women. After all, [groom] chose [bride] ... but [bride] chose [groom].'

'And what about those wonderful bridesmaids? You look fantastic ... as do all the other ladies here today. Now [groom] has finally tied the knot, I suppose the time has come for me, too, to take a wife. The only question remains: whose wife to take?'

ROAST THE GROOM

This is where you go up a gear. If you decide to include a couple of stories, keep them short. People will soon lose interest if you drone on and on. It's safer to give them roasts and jokes based on his job, interests, looks, character traits. Write a few of these down and devise your material around them. You are presenting a verbal caricature here, so everything you say must have a ring of truth about it to be funny.

Let's assume groomie is a lazy, follicly-challenged armchair sportsman and occasional dodgy second-hand car dealer. (Why on earth did she choose *him*?) You might say:

'We were down the car lot last weekend when [groom] pointed to an old Escort. "I can't shift this," he said, "I'll have to reduce it." "By how much?" I asked. "Oh, by about three owners and 50,000 miles." I'm not surprised he can't sell anything though ... he's never there ... prefers to take a sickie, lounge around and watch sport on the box all day. He's going to hospital shortly to have something removed from his backside ... his chair. But have some sympathy, his old football injury is acting up again. It happened two seasons ago. He was watching Match of the Day when he accidentally cut his thumb on a can of Holstein Pils. What a hair-raising moment that must have been ... oops, sorry [groom].'

PRAISE THE GROOM

I'm afraid it has to be done. Don't worry though – a cheesy compliment can always be followed by a cheeky put-down or two.

'Joking aside, [groom] is a great guy. My best friend. [Bride] you are lucky to have married him. He is a man of hidden talents ... I just hope some day he'll find them.' 'No, only kidding. [Groom] is a wonderful human being – a man of unique strengths and qualities ... maybe we can cryogenically freeze him until scientists find a cure.

Seriously though, [bride] is lucky to have found a lad like [groom]. It is an honour and privilege to be able to call him my friend. He has so much going for him. We call him Mr Reliable because he's so responsible ... if anything goes wrong it's odds on he's responsible. And he doesn't know the meaning of the word Tight-fistedness. Mind you, he doesn't know the meaning of lots of other words either.'

COMPLIMENT THE BRIDE

A few kind words about the bride will never go amiss. Keep any follow-up humour mild and to a minimum. After all, it's *her* big day and an unqualified compliment or two is sure to be appreciated. Try to come up with a couple in advance based on her personal circumstances or personality traits ('hard working', 'dependable', 'considerate', and so on). But be prepared to substitute or add a few topical references on the big day ('beautiful dress', 'lovely flowers', 'magnificent speech', or whatever).

> 'I'm sure we'll all agree, [bride] looks radiant today ... and those gorgeous flowers were something else. We are all delighted that your difficult year has ended on such a wonderful, positive note.

> Since I have got to know [bride] well over the last few months I have been amazed how much she does to help friends and family. I wouldn't have thought there were enough hours in the day ... but you manage it - superbly. On behalf of everyone, I thank you. You deserve all the happiness in the world - and with [groom] you are sure to find it.

> And wasn't that dress amazing? [Bride], everyone is so proud of you. First-class honours and now a first-class male. What follows is sure to be a first-class life.'

CONGRATULATE THE HAPPY COUPLE

Keep the tone serious and sincere for a little longer. This unexpected change of style and presentation in what has otherwise been a light-hearted, jokey speech will work wonders for you. There won't be a dry eye in the house. You could even weave in a short quotation or poem if it suits the particular background and circumstances of the newly-weds.

'[Groom] has been a great friend to me through thick and thin and I am delighted he has found [bride] ... and she is equally lucky to have met [groom]. They met at the tennis club and are now game and set to make the perfect match ... a lifelong love game with no tie-breaks.'

'We wish you all the happiness in the world. You are two wonderful people and you deserve each other. As teachers, you know one plus one equals two. Well, usually. In the arithmetic of love, one plus one equals everything and two minus one equals nothing. We wish you everything.'

'I am delighted you found each other after all the troubles and difficulties you've both faced over the last few years. I would like to share this thought with you: "Wedlock's not properly judged till the second glass."'

OFFER A FEW PEARLS OF WISDOM

It's back to comedy mode. You are now expected to proffer some advice to the newly-weds. Leave any really serious or emotional stuff to the bride's father, or to the groom, if they're that way inclined.

'Keep your fridge full of beer and keep all your ups and downs underneath the covers.'

'Advice to the bridegroom? Easy. When she hands you a dishcloth, blow your nose on it and hand it back.'

'It is important to establish the ground rules early in a marriage. On the first night of our honeymoon, I took off my trousers, tossed them to [your wife] and said, "Put them on."'

She gave me a funny look, stepped into them and said "well?"
I said, "That, my love, is the first and last time you wear the
trousers in this marriage." She took my trousers off, dropped
her knickers and threw them at me. She said, "Put them on." I
said, "I'll _never_ get into them." She said, "No, and until you
change your attitude, sweetheart, you never will."'

READ THE MESSAGES

This is a good time to read messages from people who couldn't be
there in person. You may have a combination of letters, cards,
e-mails, texts and other telemessages to get through. Keep things
interesting by providing a few background details about the people
who sent them (not just 'Uncle Tom' but '[Groom's] 80-year-old
Uncle Tom from South Africa, who decided to emigrate on the day
he first met [groom]').

Try to end on a particularly high note. Perhaps with the funniest or
most emotional message, with one from relatives who live on the
other side of the world, or with one from some very old family
friends (in either or preferably both senses of the phrase).
Alternatively, you could _make up_ the final message. However, if you
do this, it should be obvious to everyone that it's a joke.

'And finally, this one is from that old quill-pusher, William
Shakespeare. And it says, "Sorry that I can't be with you
today, but I'm Bard." Snakey goes on, "It hath been said that
all unhappy marriages are a result of a husband having brains."
Verily, I have total confidence that this marriage will be an
exceptionally happy one.'

'And the final message comes from serial husband Henry VIII. It says, "Congratulations to you both. This is the happiest day of your lives ... and good luck for your wedding tomorrow."'

'This last one comes from the girls at [bride's work, local, sports club, etc.]. It says, "There were three crucial stages to your ceremony today:

The aisle – the longest walk you'll ever take
The altar – the place where two became one
The hymn – the choral celebration of marriage.

[Bride], please repeat after me: "Aisle, Altar, Hymn ... Aisle, Altar, Hymn ..."'

BIG FINISH AND TOAST

A wedding speech is like a love affair. Any fool can start one but to end it requires considerable skill. If you can find the ideal ending, you will inject that ultimate bit of magic. In the same way that your opening remarks should include both an attention-grabbing hook and a short response on behalf of the bridesmaids, so your final words (not literally, I trust) should include both a memorable closing line and a toast to the happy couple. Here are some possibilities, but, as always, try to be personal, relevant and original.

'May the best day of your past be the worst day of your future. Ladies and Gentlemen – friends – please join me in a toast: The bride and groom.'

'I leave you with this thought ... there are Seven Deadly Sins, enough for one each day. Have a great week's honeymoon.

Ladies and Gentlemen, a toast: The bride and groom.'

'I must close now because of my throat .... [wife/girlfriend] told me that if I went on for more than ten minutes, she would cut it. So in the interests of my health, let's all drink a toast to their health. Ladies and Gentlemen: Here's to the health and happiness of ...'

'As I said to the woman I lost my virginity to, thanks for laughing. Ladies and Gentlemen, please raise your glasses. Let's drink a toast to ...'

And thank *you* for laughing ... if you did. Now you've got all the ammunition you need, it's time to start thinking about writing your speech.

Writing Your Speech

Almost there now, bestie. You know all the broad areas you are going to cover … and you've got plenty of ideas of personal, relevant and original things you could say in each of them. You haven't? Well rewind to Chapter 6 until you have … I don't want to have to put you in the Naughty Corner. You're back. Great. Now it's time to get ruthless as you start to put it all together.

CHOOSE YOUR MATERIAL

Go through each section of your skeleton outline and decide which ideas have the X Factor and which ones are destined for the delete button. It won't be as difficult as it sounds because by now deep down you will *know* your strongest material. Trust your instinct. If you are still unsure, ask yourself the four questions that the late and great Bob Monkhouse devised for vetting all his potential material:

Do *you* think it is funny or meaningful?

You will always deliver a funny line better when you genuinely like it. If you're not totally happy about a gag or story, you can be sure that your subconscious mind is warning you not to use it. Follow this showbiz adage: If in doubt, leave it out.

Can you say it confidently and with comfort?

Is this story right for you? If you are a natural wit (I said wit) and a bit of an extrovert, you may feel fine telling a joke that requires a mastery of accents, perfect timing, expressive gestures and practised articulation for a tongue-twisting punchline. If you are a mere mortal, think twice – and then several more times, before taking any unnecessary risks with stuff like this. Your speech is a one-shot deal. Know your limitations.

Is it inoffensive?

A great deal of specious claptrap is spoken about 'honest vulgarity' as opposed to filth. I have never been convinced there is any difference. Yes, fashions have changed and what is acceptable in a wedding speech today would have been unthinkable just a few years ago. But never overstep that unspoken, invisible line. This is a family occasion. Remember your audience. Have a serious go at the groom but don't swear or be vindictive towards him. If you are, you will come over as bitchy, bitter and bereft of humour and humanity.

Will they understand and appreciate it?

Remember that all your material should be personal, relevant and original. It must be *meaningful* to your audience given the circumstances, backgrounds, lifestyles and characteristics of the newly-weds. The funniest joke in the world about an MP in a cave will have no place in your speech unless the bride or groom are political potholers.

If a gag or story gets a thumbs-up to all these questions, it will merit a place in your speech.

GET CREATIVE?

The original fail-safe structure of your speech might do the job for you. Alternatively, you may decide to do a little tweaking here and there – perhaps changing the order of components, merging the contents of some of them, or adding something completely new. My only advice is not to tamper unless you have a good reason to do so. To make structural changes to improve and personalise your speech is highly creative; to make them just to be different is foolish.

You may decide to include a few props – such as enlarged embarrassing photos of the groom – or even get some of the audience to act as confederates for one of your jokes. That's fine … so long as the gag's *original*. The first time I saw the 'key joke' on *You've Been Framed*, I thought it was very funny. The best man says something along the lines of: 'I know [groom] had some girlfriends during his bachelor days and I see a few of them here today. I've been asked if any still have a key to his front door that they return it now …' Cue a long line of females running to throw a key into a large tin. Many of your audience will have seen this clip rerun on TV many times and also played out at other weddings. Please don't copy any visual joke you have seen on the box or found online. *You* may find it hilarious … *they* will find it monotonous.

KEEP IT FLOWING

Have you noticed how entertainers, politicians and TV presenters move easily and unobtrusively from one topic to another? Like them, you can make your speech flow smoothly and gracefully from beginning to end by putting your sections into a logical order and then joining them together with *link words* and *bridging lines*.

Link words are words or short phrases – like *meanwhile, however, anyway, mind you* and *of course* – that allow you to move seamlessly from line to line. **Bridging lines** are phrases and sentences that allow you to move on to another section or topic in an *apparently* natural and conversational manner.

Let's take an example. Here's how you could link a few jokes about the groom's early years before bridging to his enjoyment of the good life today. The link words are underlined and the bridging lines are indicated.

Okay [groom] was a bit of a slow starter. It's true. He could never understand why his sister had three brothers and he only had two. not only that, at Playschool he was different from the other five-year olds ... he was 11. Mind you, he went to a very good school ... must have been ... he told me it was approved. By the age of 14, though, his parents were getting concerned about his performance there. He wasn't just falling behind ... he was getting lapped. That's right ... friends used to ask [his parents] what they thought he'd be when he left school. The usual reply was, 'An old-age pensioner.'

[Bridging line] But eventually he did leave [name of school] and became a gifted amateur magician ...

Oh yes, he can be walking down a street and just turn into a pub. Mind you he's not only a brilliant magician, he does amazing impressions too ... he eats like a pig and drinks like a fish. Don't know why he asked me to be best man today really ... his best mates are Jack Daniels and Johnnie Walker ... and his idea of a balanced meal is a Big Mac in each hand.

You know, [bride] tells me the first time she set her eyes on [groom], she thought he was handsome from afar ... now she just thinks he's far from handsome ... [Bridging line].

Come on, looks aren't everything ... fortunately for [groom] ... etc. ... etc. ... etc.

USE WORDS TO BE SAID, NOT READ

Most people can write something to be *read*, few can write something to be *said*. Indeed, most people are unaware that there is any difference.

We are used to writing things to be read: by our friends, our relatives, our work colleagues. Such everyday written communication is known as **text**. What we are *not* used to doing is speaking our written words out loud. Writing intended to be spoken and heard is known as **script**.

Every effective speaker *must* recognise that there are very important differences between text and script, namely:

Text	Script
is a journey at the reader's pace	is a journey at the speaker's pace
can be reread, if necessary	is heard once, and only once
can be read in any order	is heard in the order it is spoken
should be grammatically correct	need not be grammatically correct
should not be conversational	should be conversational

Therefore, you must prepare a speech for an audience which *cannot* listen at its own pace; which *cannot* ask you to repeat parts it did not hear or understand; and which *cannot* choose the order in which to consider your words. Think like a listener and write like a talker. The style and tone of your script should be relaxed and chatty.

Consider how the same gag might be put over, first using text and then script:

Text: 'I first met [bride] some seven years ago and I've been very friendly with [groom] for eight years longer than that. During this time I have witnessed some terrible haircuts and silly moustaches. Over the years [groom] has made a few mistakes in that department as well.'

Script: 'I've known [bride] for around seven years and have been now more or less best mates with [groom] for about 15 ... as you can imagine, I've seen some right dodgy haircuts and some real nightmare moustaches ... mind you, [groom's] not always got it right either.'

The lesson is clear: **speak your words out loud before you commit them to paper.**

PREPARE YOUR SCRIPT

The best talkers are those who are most natural. They are easy, fluent, friendly and amusing. No script for them. How could there be? They are talking only to us and basing what they say on our reactions as they go along. For most of us, however, that sort of performance is an aspiration rather than a description. Our tongues are not so honeyed and our words less winged. We need a script.

But what sort of a script? Cards? Notes? Speech written out in full? There is no right way of doing it. Here is a simple method favoured by many speakers:

1. Write out the speech **in full**.

2. **Memorise** the opening and closing lines and **familiarise** yourself with the remainder of the speech.

3. **Summarise** the speech on one sheet of paper using **key words** to remind you of your **sequence** of jokes, anecdotes and so on.

The main advantage of this method is that you will not only be sure to cover everything you want to, but also will come across as a natural and spontaneous speaker who is not merely reciting a prepared speech.

Making Your Speech

This chapter is not about making *a* speech or making *the* speech … it is about making **your** speech. In other words, it is about presenting your material in such a way that your unique personality shines through. Did Elvis, Sinatra and Johnny Rotten all sound the same singing *My Way*? Of course not. The artist makes the crucial difference. So, too, does the speaker.

FIND YOUR STYLE

We are not clones. We are individuals with wonderful imperfections. Whatever individual characteristics you have that are special to you should be nurtured and cultivated and worked on, for it is those personal and unique quirks of appearance, movement and expression that will mark you out as a speaker with something different to offer. And that is never a bad thing.

Be conversational

Sitting at leisure with friends or family, your conversation will be naturally relaxed and chatty, because that is the language of easy communication. When you make your speech, don't put on an act. If you do you will come over as phoney, boring and insincere. Certainly you may need to speak a little louder than usual and make other concessions to accommodate the needs of your audience. Yet the way you deliver your speech should remain unaffectedly relaxed and chatty. Be yourself – but yourself made large.

Casual conversation is not constructed in a literary way. You do not always finish your sentences. You repeat yourself. You use ungrammatical constructions – but you are obeying a different set of rules. You are obeying the rules of effective spoken communication which have been learnt, instinctively, down the ages. Don't abandon them when you speak in public.

Be heard

You must be audible. If you are not, all else is lost. If there is public address equipment available, find out how it works – if possible get some practice before the big day – and then use it. If there is no sound-enhancing equipment, speak as clearly and as loudly as is necessary to be heard. If the only other person in the room was at the back, you would talk to him or her naturally, at the right level, without shouting or strain, by:

► Keeping your head up
► Opening your mouth wider than during everyday speech
► Speaking more clearly
► Slowing down

If you remember that you must be heard by that same person, at the back, during your speech, however many other people may be in the room, you will make those same four natural adjustments to your delivery.

Give out the right non-verbal messages

We *speak* with our vocal cords, but we *communicate* with our whole body. An audience does a lot more than listen to a speech – it *experiences* it. Everything about a speaker's manner and demeanour contributes to the overall impression that the audience takes away.

So what hidden messages are you giving when you speak? If you are unsure, watch yourself in a mirror, get someone to video you with a mobile, or ask a kind but critical friend what they think. You will probably find it would be useful to work on one or more of the following:

► Stance and posture
► Movement and gestures
► Eye contact and facial expression

While it is vital not to put on an act, it is important to learn to project yourself as positively as you can … and a positive change made to any one of these areas will also have a direct and immediate positive effect on the others.

Stance and posture
Your stance and posture are important. You are making a fundamental statement with your body. An aligned, upright posture conveys a message of confidence and integrity. In Chapter 1 we talked about your great-great-(and about another 50 greats)-grandfather. He frightened his enemies by inflating his chest, spreading his arms and clenching his fists to appear a macho man. Don't frighten the guests by impersonating him. A friendly, upright open stance is far preferable. When the old boy was being attacked, he would put a shield between himself and his foes. If you cross your arms you will be perceived as defending yourself from the audience. Open arms and open palms are seen as friendly and positive.

Movement and gestures
When your beloved ancestor got into a ruck with the lads in the next village, he would first make confidence-boosting 'bring it on' gestures

to them. If any were foolish enough to accept his invitation, he would hold a club above his head before bringing it down with great force onto theirs. Our legacy from this is that, even today, pointing and finger-wagging are seen as extremely hostile gestures. To come over as the friendly and unthreatening chappie you undoubtedly are, you should try to keep your fingers pointing downward.

Eye contact and facial expression

These are crucial aspects of effective communication because they gain and then maintain an audience's attention, create rapport and give you valuable feedback as to how well you are coming over. So look all around the room as you speak. Everyone must be included. If the folks at the back get the impression you are having a private party with your buddies at the front, they will soon switch off.

But you must do more than simply look at your audience. You must use your eyes and facial expression to convey your *feelings*. It isn't as difficult as it may sound. You do it every day. As always, support your words with looks that convey happiness, optimism, mirth, joy, confidence, sincerity.

There is nothing more captivating than a genuine smile. It shows warmth and friendliness and says, 'I'm really pleased to be making this speech. It's going to be great fun … and my mate is going to wish he'd never been born.' So smile, smile – and smile again.

Telling jokes and stories

It is exceedingly difficult to discuss technique in general terms, since the telling of funny stories is such a personal business. My only advice is: Be yourself and don't go on for too long. Tell the story logically and get to the meat of the gag quickly.

The precise wording and style of delivery of a joke or story, of course, must be *yours*, not mine. If you are a naturally funny person, that's great. Give it plenty of wellie. But don't worry if you are not a born comic. You can still win your laughs – by playing it straight. For many of us the best way to tell a joke is seriously. Smile most of the time but act out your gags with deadpan expressions. It's a no-lose approach. They will probably find it hilarious … if they don't laugh when you expected them to, they won't know they should have.

But we all have *some* abilities and talents. Don't hide your light under a bushel. Any regional accents or dialects which you can do well (and only if you *can* do them well) should be incorporated into your stories. A punchline is doubled in effect in the appropriate Cockney or Brummie accent – especially after a straight and serious build-up. The important thing is to be *yourself* and tell jokes in the way *you* find easiest and most comfortable.

MAKE FEAR YOUR FRIEND

Fear is nothing to be frightened of. People get nervous because they are afraid of failing, of looking foolish and not living up to expectations. Nervousness is caused by the fear of looking ridiculous to others.

Few speakers claim to be able to speak without any nerves. Most will say that lack of nerves is not only unlikely, it is undesirable. They need the adrenaline to carry them along. So how can you make things easier for yourself? First be assured that excessive worry is avoidable, if you follow these top tips:

Rehearse

Rehearse the beginning and ending until you have them spot on. Rehearse the rest of your speech not to be perfect but to be *comfortable*. An audience won't expect you to be perfect – in fact they won't give a damn if you fluff a line or two. They are on your side and willing you to do well. However, they *need* you to be comfortable. If you are not comfortable, neither are they. And if they're not comfortable, they *cannot* enjoy the moment, however hard they may try.

Why do some actors freeze or fumble on the opening night and pick up an award three months later? It's a fear of unfamiliarity. As days, weeks and months go by, the fear abates, confidence soars and the quality of performance improves beyond recognition. Words become more familiar. Awkward phrases are smoothed out. You suddenly think of a way of saying a stuffy sentence in a more straightforward and colloquial style. At the same time, you will recognise the parts of your speech that hit the spot, the parts that require a little fine tuning, and the parts that are simply not worth including.

Rehearse in the way that best suits you. Some speakers like to be isolated and unheard. Others perform their speeches again and again to a sympathetic friend, either encouraging suggestions from them or requiring nothing more than a repeated hearing, to ease away inhibitions. Once you have confidence in your material and have practised until you can get through it without a lot of 'umming' and 'er-ing', you will be ready to belt it out without a seeming care in the world.

Have the right mental attitude

Tell yourself you are going to make a great little speech. And *believe* it. The largely untapped power of positive thinking really is enormous. About 85% of performance is directly related to attitude. This may sound like American claptrap. It isn't. Attitude is everything.

A final thought before you stand and deliver (please read it out loud time and time again): Whether you think you will succeed or whether you think you will fail, you will probably be right.

SAMPLE SPEECHES

Sample Speeches

Finally, it's time to take a look at some full-length speeches. If you find a line or two that suit your needs, that's fine. But please don't crib too much. And if you do borrow anything, adapt and personalise it so it becomes unrecognisable from the original. In that way, no one will be aware of your source … or your sauce. The last thing I want to do is to encourage an assembly line of suits each regurgitating similar or even identical speeches. You owe it to the happy couple – and to yourself – to make your speech original, personal and relevant to them. So prepare a *unique* speech and – when you stand and deliver – try to add a few topical comments about the highlights or funnier moments of the day.

The main purpose for including these ten samples is not to provide you with ready-made material; it is to remind you of the style and tone you should adopt. Your speech should be upbeat, congratulatory, humorous … and *short*. Each of the speeches that follow would take no more than ten minutes to deliver. Don't make the mistake of starting your speech at one o'clock *sharp* and ending it at two o'clock *dull*. Leave them wanting more.

Here's the deal: Darren has just married Laura and the best man is Neil. Their personalities, characteristics, interests – and the names of their friends and relatives will vary from speech to speech. In Speech 9, Neil is joined by Scott and in the final speech, Neil becomes Julie (well, it's good to have a hobby).

SAMPLE SPEECH 1

Can everyone at the back hear me? Yeah? Okay, mine's a pint. Good afternoon, Ladies, Gentlemen and those of uncertain gender. Now I'm going to keep this short because, quite honestly, it's cutting into my Saturday afternoon cricket time ... I should be standing in the slips now with my legs apart waiting for a little tickle. But we must all make sacrifices.

My name is Neil and, as is customary at this stage, on behalf of the most beautiful set of bridesmaids I have ever set my eyes on, I would like to thank Darren for his kind words and generous gifts. I'm not sure why they can't thank him themselves ... but there we go. And didn't the ushers do a great job, too? It's not easy being an usher. I was one at a mate's wedding recently and I asked a lady who was entering the church whether she was a friend of the groom. 'Most certainly not, young man,' she replied, 'I'm the bride's mother.'

Just before I start [*big yawn*] ... Sorry, in the early hours of this morning, Darren insisted on one final visit to the Golden Triangle Massage Parlour. I waited outside for him ... but it was still a late night for both of us. Anyway, I'm honoured to be standing up here today. I'm sure a lot of you guys out there have been asked to be a best man yourselves. But I bet none of you have received written guidelines from the bride-to-be. About a fortnight ago, I did. I received this e-mail from Laura. Let me read it to you:

'I'm so pleased you have agreed to be Darren's best man. I'm sure you'll be fantastic. But could I politely ask you not to say or do anything that would spoil our wedding day? With this in mind, kindly take note of the following and we'll all be sure to have a great time ...

1. Don't get drunk

2. Don't swear or tell dirty jokes

3. Don't use your fingers when eating

4. Don't take food from anyone else's plate

5. Don't pick your nose or scratch your bum

6. Don't discuss Darren's little problem

7. Don't leer at women with low-cut tops

8. Don't harass the bridesmaids

9. Don't steal anything

10. But most importantly, enjoy yourself … but not too much.'

Thank you Laura, very comprehensive. I hope you will agree I've followed your advice to the letter … so far. I think my first job – getting Darren to the church on time and sober – was a complete success … I'm sure he'll be fine when the Valium wears off. Now it's time for my second major task – to tell you a few little secrets about our groom. Where shall I begin? Well, I've known him since we first played cricket together at Primary School. He's handsome, intelligent, witty … sorry, wrong speech.

Darren was born back in 1976. Now I don't know if it's a coincidence or not, but a couple of weeks after he was born Family Planning was made available free on the National Health. At the age of four he was packed off to nursery. On the first day his teacher showed him how to put his shoes on by himself. But then she noticed that the left shoe was on the right foot. She said, 'Darren, your shoes are on the wrong feet.' He looked at her with a raised brow and said 'Don't be silly, Miss, I know they're my feet' … bright kid. Then came school … here's his Year Ten report. Let me read it to you. 'Darren is an ideal pupil who excels in most subjects' … oops, I got that a bit wrong … it actually says, 'Darren is an idle student who's been expelled in most subjects.' But seriously, he's always been a great friend to me … a real mate … he's special … at least that's what our school psychologist called him.

Over the last couple of weeks I've been talking to lots of you to help form a broader, more balanced view of the man. When I heard words like ignorant, conceited and lazy, I thought, hang on, that's a bit rough … but if his parents don't know him, who does? None of you will know this, but I've actually congratulated the groom in private already. 'Darren,' I said, 'you will always look back on this day as the happiest and best thing you have ever done.' Fitting words, I thought, at the end of a fantastic stag weekend.

Laura, you look magnificent. I know things have been a little rough for you over the last few months. Darren loves you terribly … but, with time and practice, he's sure to improve. It's funny how history repeats itself … 25 years ago Laura's mum and dad were sending her to bed with a dummy … and here we go again …

I asked Darren what he was looking for in this marriage. He thought carefully for a few moments and then said, 'Love, happiness and … eventually a family.' When I asked Laura the same question, without hesitation she replied, 'A coffee percolator.' Well actually she said a perky copulator … but I knew what she meant. Laura is a lovely lady … and we are all so proud of the wonderful work she does for sick animals ... it was while she was helping out at the vets that she first met Darren ... he was taking his dog for an injection. The poor old animal had an injection every week for a year after that ... just so Darren had an excuse to talk to Laura.

But in all seriousness, I am absolutely delighted that Darren and Laura have decided to spend the rest of their lives together. You couldn't have chosen a nicer church, a nicer reception room ... or a nicer best man. Now, as is customary, I'll offer a couple of pearls of wisdom for you to ponder ...

Laura ... Treat Darren like a dog ... three meals a day, plenty of affection ... and send him into the garden for a wee before bedtime.

Darren ... Never get complacent. Look out for those tell-tale signs that there may be something wrong in your relationship ... you know, like the postman wearing your socks.

Now before I wind up, I'd like to read a few messages from some people who couldn't make it here today.

[*Read the genuine messages*]

This is the final one:

'Saturday evenings will never be the same again. We wish you happiness in your new life, but how we'll miss you, Big Boy. From all the girls ... and boys ... at the Golden Triangle.'

But it really has been brilliant seeing Darren relaxing and letting his hair down this afternoon … for the past couple of years, it's been his hair that's been letting him down. In all seriousness though, Darren, you've been a brilliant friend – and a crappy batsman – over the years. It's been a real honour to be your best man today. You certainly bowled this maiden over. Laura, you are a lovely lady. We are all familiar with your many virtues … your tenacity, your sunny disposition, your great love of dumb animals … no prizes for guessing the main beneficiary of that last one. With all my heart I wish you both a long and incredibly happy marriage together. You deserve it. Ladies and Gentlemen, please raise your glasses. A toast … the bride and groom.

SAMPLE SPEECH 2

Thank you, Darren, for that generous introduction ... wonderfully restrained, I thought. Good afternoon, Ladies and Gentlemen. For those of you who don't know me, my name is Neil, and yes, I'm the one who drew the short straw ... sorry, was given the honour of being Darren's best man ... No, I was absolutely delighted to be asked to do the business for him ... and I think it shows what this honour means to me, because I had to let my girlfriend down to be here today. Not to worry though, I can blow her back up again when I get home.

As is customary, I'm about to say a few words about the groom ... Don't worry, folks, I won't talk for too long ... Laura tells me she is used to Darren performing for 30 seconds or less, so I don't want to outperform him. Let's make a deal ... the more you laugh, the faster I'll deliver the speech.

But first, I want to say a huge thanks on behalf of all us attendants to Darren for his kind words to us all. I'd like to add my own congratulations to the bridesmaids for helping Laura get ready and for making sure she got to the church on time – well almost on time. No mean feat as I understand she put up quite a struggle. Frankly, I thought you would have made more of the opportunity and spoken for longer ... Darren, now you're a married man you won't get many more chances like that to talk without interruption.

You know, it's turning out to be a day packed with new experiences for me. It's the first time I've had the honour of being a best man ... it's the first time that Darren has complimented me in all the years I've known him ... and it's the first time I've got a free meal out of

him since that kebab he bought me in 1997 to celebrate my 18th ...
Darren, I met Liz last week and yesterday she became my 53rd.

But I must say, Laura, you look truly stunning today. I think the word
'radiant' would not be an overstatement. You always have such a
genuine smile that it makes everyone around you want to smile too.
Darren, you look like you always do ... third prize in the raffle. No
seriously, you've scrubbed up quite nicely ... but I'm not too pleased
about you copying my outfit.

The purpose of a best man's speech, or so I've been told, is to
embarrass the groom ... well Darren has a small willy, picks his nose
and subscribes to *Big and Bouncy* magazine ... and I think that is
quite embarrassing enough. Final offer, Darren twenty quid to skip
the rugby bit? No? Okay, here goes He used to play rugby for our
school, but it soon became apparent his tackle just wasn't big
enough ... not even for mini-rugby.

So what can I tell you about Darren that hasn't already appeared in
an episode of the *Jerry Springer Show* or *Neighbours from Hell*? This can
be no more than a short and superficial review of his life and exploits
to date. Anyone requiring more comprehensive coverage should
refer to pages 4 to 7 of tomorrow's *News of the World* ... and yes, that
is a goat ... and no, I didn't realise it was physically possible to do
that either.

To be fair though, Darren could be described as charming, witty,
entertaining ... and perhaps one day he will be. Don't worry, mate
... I won't mention what special name your mum and dad had for
you. I won't mention what Little Willy, sorry Darren did that

scandalised the neighbours, and whatever he's done with rubber chickens is in the past … well, that's his own business … that's not an aspect of his life I want to talk about today … not in such nice company.

Starting at the beginning … Darren was born just around the corner from here 29 years ago. He was so surprised by his birth that he was speechless for about a year and a half. Actually, his mum tells me he came prematurely … so nothing new there then, eh Laura? Now I'm not saying he was an ugly baby, but Mary used to put a bone around his neck, so the dog would play with him.

I asked his dad if he had any cute photos of Darren which I could show today. There was this really sweet one of him lying on a sheepskin rug playing with his little organ … he's always been a very musical chap … I was going to have it blown up to show you today, but then I thought it might be too embarrassing because it was only taken last year.

I was first introduced to Darren at school by Sam, our mutual friend who is sadly here today. My first impression of Darren was a guy with a really distinctive fashion sense. He always stood out from the crowd. Before too long, he became my role model and I started to copy the sorts of things he used to wear – until my mother grounded me for taking clothes from her wardrobe.

But in all sincerity, in many ways Darren has been a role model for me … he's reliable, trustworthy, hard-working … well, to sum him up … he's a nice bloke. Laura, you couldn't have done any better. And Darren, you couldn't have done any better choosing Laura either … you two were meant for each other … and I want to say how absolutely delighted I am that you two have finally tied the knot. You are two of my best mates and I am over the moon for you both.

As you probably know, it is customary for a best man to impart a few pearls of wisdom to the happy couple This seems somewhat bizarre to me as I'm not married myself. But anyway, here goes …

Laura, remember that men are like fine wine … they start off as grapes and it's your job to relentlessly stamp on them until they turn into something you would like to have dinner with.

Darren, women are also like fine wine … they start out fresh, fruity and intoxicating to the mind … turn full bodied with age … and finally become all sour and vinegary …

But seriously, after seeing my parents I can tell you marriage really is like wine … it gets better with age.

Before I bring this to a close, here are some messages from people who couldn't make it here today…

[*Read the genuine messages*]

And here's the last one:

To Darren, a loyal and valued customer … our best wishes to you and your bride. PS: Will you be renewing your subscription? Regards, *Big and Bouncy* magazine.

So, in conclusion, how can I sum up Darren to you? A successful businessman? A talented dancer? A gifted footballer? Darren is in fact none of these. However, I'm sure he will be a brilliant husband. It's wonderful to see you making this commitment to each other. Darren, you are a lucky man to have found Laura … and Laura, you are a lucky woman to have found Darren.

Marriage in this day and age is far from easy. With all the pressures of day-to-day living, you will need to grow in mutual trust and understanding without ever forgetting what first brought you together. In other words, may your love be modern enough to survive the times, yet old-fashioned enough to last forever. Ladies and Gentlemen, a toast: to Little Willy … I mean to Darren and Laura.

SAMPLE SPEECH 3

Good evening everyone, my name is Neil and I'm an alcoholic ... oops, that's Wednesdays. Ladies and Gentlemen, Boys and Girls, for those of you who don't know me, my name is Neil and I'm Darren's lighter ... sorry, younger brother. It probably won't come as a surprise to you that I've known him all my life. And during all that time, he's been ... well, like a brother to me. I guess you all know what brothers can be like to one another ... constant arguments, threats and even fights over whose the best man ... then, about six months ago, Darren took me to one side and finally conceded it was me. And as undisputed best man, it is my privilege, on behalf of all the attendants, to thank Big Bruv for his kind words. Actually, he didn't have any kind words for me so I'll take that bit back.

Weren't the bridesmaids wonderful today? Where did you learn to pout, look pretty and hold flowers all at the same time? I can't even look pretty when I'm not doing anything else. Well, as tradition demands, on behalf of these multi-tasking young ladies, I thank you, Darren, for your most generous words about them. I agree: they were magnificent. And doesn't the bride look incredible today? She truly is the star of the show. Laura, here's to you. As for Darren, well what can I say, we tried our best.

Well, what a day it's been ... the car wouldn't start ... piston broke.... that's the story of my life ... Rose and Andy couldn't find the church ... Steve bought a round ... whatever next? But it's been an amazing few hours. I think you'll all agree that the ceremony was really moving ... especially when Darren said 'I do' ... to which Laura added, 'You'd better.' And the food here has been out of this world. I think we should raise our glasses to the caterers ... any excuse for a drink.

I'll let you into a little secret. In the run-up to today Darren and Laura had a bit of a difference of opinion over the seating plan for the meal … they just couldn't agree on who should sit where. So as best man, I offered to step in to find a mutually acceptable solution. What we finally came up with was to use the wedding present list, and to put those of you who bought the biggest items nearest the front and work back from there. So if they can hear me at the back there, thank you to Dave and Sue for that out-of-code jar of pickled onions.

As many of you will already know, Darren and I share a passion in life for the beautiful game … you just can't beat 90 minutes of running around in the open air, half-naked on a Saturday afternoon … and we both love our football too. Darren thinks he's a natural … just because he's been able to kick, spit and dribble since he was a baby. But he's not as good as he thinks he is, though. When a chap donated a quid to our club last season, the manager said, 'For that, you can take Darren … and don't forget your 50 pence change.'

But Darren is more than just a crap footballer … he's crap at so many other things as well. When we were at school, he asked his music teacher for her honest opinions of his compositions. She looked at him straight in the eye and said, 'I believe your songs will be played when Beethoven and the Beatles are forgotten … but not before.'

I've heard he's not 100% when it comes to you-know-what either. Soon after they'd announced their engagement, Laura told Darren that she wanted to make love every night of the week. Darren thought about this for a moment or two and then replied, 'That's wonderful, love … you can pencil me in for Fridays and every other Tuesday.'

Turning from the ridiculous to the sublime … doesn't Laura look brilliant? You're a great girl and you deserve all the happiness in the world. With Darren, I am confident you will find it. You know, these two have it all. Individually they are successful … together they can accomplish anything. There is no stopping them now … unless, of course, Darren's court hearing goes the wrong way … No, I didn't realise it was illegal to wash your privates in the loo in McDonalds either.

But honestly, you two were meant to be together … your man and your woman … your Romeo and your Juliet … your yin and your yang. It's as natural as his and her bath mats. It's been a bit of a musical day one way and another … violins in harmony with cellos … Laura in harmony with Darren … the past in harmony with the future. And, as the Bard of Avon put it, 'If music be the food of love … rock on.'

Now as best man, I have the opportunity to offer some advice to the happy couple. Incidentally, for those of you who don't know, I'm not actually married myself … I just look like this because I've been unwell recently. But I'm sure the right girl for me is just round the corner … unless the police have moved her on since last night …

Anyway, here goes …

Darren: nurture your marriage the same way you nurture your beloved football … be fully committed, plan to score mid-week and every Saturday … and always change ends at half time.

Laura: if you ever find him playing away from home, give him a serious groin injury and put him straight onto the transfer market. Remind him there are plenty of substitutes out there.

Now it's time for me to read some e-mails, cards and letters received from absent friends:

[*Read the genuine messages*]

And finally, this one is for Laura and it comes from the lads at Darren's soccer club:

'Congratulations, Laura. We've tried Darren in several different positions and he's useless in all of them ... we wish you better luck.'

Today, I feel like I'm gaining a sister and losing a brother. I have such a mixture of emotions ... happiness, joy ... relief. But seriously, you know, it's a rare opportunity to have such a public opportunity to tell your brother how much you love him, and that is what I say to you now, Darren. You know, success in marriage is more than finding the right person ... it is being the right person. There can be no doubt that you are the right people for each other. And I really would like to say that I am delighted that Big Bruv has married Laura. We couldn't be happier that you are joining our little clan. And Laura, I'm free on Mondays and Wednesdays.

Well if my throat was dry when I started this speech, it's even drier now ... and I can think of no better remedy than to drink to the health, wealth and eternal happiness of the newly-weds. So, please raise your glasses and join me as we drink a toast to the bride and groom ... the bride and groom.

SAMPLE SPEECH 4

I always thought it would be difficult to follow a speech made by Darren … and I was right … I didn't follow a damn word of it. Good afternoon, Ladies and Gentlemen. For those of you who don't know me, my name is Neil … and for those of you who would like to know me better, my room number is 27. Firstly, on behalf of the bridesmaids, I would like to thank Darren for those kind words – they were very much appreciated. I would also echo Darren's thanks to everyone for coming today. I know that a lot of you have travelled light years to be here … it's amazing what some people will do for a free meal … but I'm sure you'll all agree it was well worth it … what a spread. The caterers have done us proud.

I stand here today as Darren's best man. His approach to asking me to fulfil this important role was, shall we say, somewhat unconventional. As far as I was concerned it was a typical Saturday evening. You know, me buying the drinks and Darren consuming them. But just before closing time, he swayed over to me, put his arm around my shoulder, burped in my face, and said, 'Well, Neil, I'm getting married soon and I guess I've got to ruin someone's day, so it might as well be yours.' Then he farted and staggered out of the pub. It was a very touching moment.

On such an illustrious occasion as this, it seems odd for me to be called best man. After all, who pays attention to a man in my position today? They all say, 'Doesn't the bride look radiant?' – which she does, and 'What a charming set of bridesmaids' – which they are, and 'What a dashing bridegroom' – which he isn't. But who says, 'What a hunk the best man is' – which, so very obviously, he is? No, if they notice me at all, they think I'm a waiter or a chauffeur. One lady here, who shall remain nameless, even asked me if my name was

Brad and had I been sent here to meet her by the Lonely Hearts Club Escort Agency? To be honest though, about a year ago I did apply to join the Lonely Hearts Club … filled in loads of forms and sent them my photo. They sent it straight back, saying they weren't that lonely. But enough of my troubles …

Before I go any further, on behalf of the bridesmaids, I'd like to thank Darren for his generous words. No problem, mate. We've all really enjoyed ourselves today. And Laura, what can I say, you look magnificent … as always. I'd better not say too much more about that or I'll be accused of chatting up a married woman … but you do look great. How well I remember the day Darren told me he'd met Laura. She had come home from uni for the weekend … I think she must have been studying in North Wales because Darren told me that from now on he'd be making a 200 mile round trip every weekend to Bangor. They had literally bumped into each other in the street. Quick as a flash, Darren said, 'If you're heart is as soft as your breast, I know you will forgive me.' To which Laura replied, 'If your knob is as hard as your elbow, here's my phone number.'

Now what can I tell you about that young man over there with the hard … elbow? Well, firstly, he's a man of rare gifts … he hasn't given one for years. But he's certainly not stupid … despite vicious and persistent rumours to the contrary. Have you noticed how few single people were invited to the wedding? I will let you into a secret … that was Darren's idea. He's very astute. He told me that if he invited only married people, all the presents would be clear profit. In all honesty though, it has to be said: a man like Darren only comes along once in a lifetime … I'm only sorry it had to be during *my* lifetime.

Oh, yes, Darren just asked me to repeat his thank yous for all your gifts. He told me Laura will find the lawn mower and electric drill particularly useful, and he will make good use of the garden hammock and the deck chairs ... Laura, you have been warned. Now I'm not saying Darren's lazy, but if it took any voluntary and sustained effort to digest his food, he would have died from lack of nourishment years ago.

But seriously, Darren is a man who knows where he's going in life ... and with Laura at his side, he is sure to get there. He's honest ... reliable ... and a man of immaculate tastes ... after all, he supports United and he chose Laura, didn't he? Laura, we know times have been difficult for you recently, but today really is the first day of the rest of your life. I couldn't be happier for you both ... you make the perfect couple.

As is customary, I will now relate a little story with a big moral that should serve Darren well throughout married life:

Picture the scene, if you will. Ten men and a woman are suspended by a rope hanging from a balloon. They are rapidly losing height and decide that one of them will need to let go of the rope or else surely they all will die. No one can decide who should go so the woman speaks up. She gives a truly eloquent and moving little speech, saying how she would make the ultimate sacrifice to save their lives. After all, women are used to giving up things for their husbands and children ... and men are the superior sex and must therefore be saved. After she had finished speaking, all the men clapped ... Darren, never underestimate the power of a woman ...

Drawing to a close, I'd like to say that you two have the sense of humour, love and support for one another necessary to help you through any difficult times ... and the courage and determination to make sure things soon go right again. As we celebrate this magnificent day, let us remember that a marriage is not just a ceremony ... it is a creation. May this couple create a wonderful world together filled with love, laughter and life ...

Now just before I make the toast, I'd like to read a few messages received from friends and family who couldn't be here with us today ...

[*Read the genuine messages*]

This is the last one:

'To Darren, We'll miss the threesomes ... Love, Jordan and Peter.'

You know, a wise man once said, 'We cannot fully enjoy life unless someone we love enjoys it with us.' Darren has found that special lady to enjoy life with. Now as a person who will drink to absolutely anything, it gives me immense pleasure to invite you all to be upstanding, raise your glasses and join me in a toast to the bride and groom, because I know they were made for each other. Ladies and Gentlemen: the bride and groom.

SAMPLE SPEECH 5

For those of you who do not know me, my name is Neil … and for those of you who do … well, I apologise. When Darren asked me to be his best man, I was initially dead chuffed at the prospect. But then I remembered the last time I had to stand up in front of a room of people … I was given an Asbo and fined fifty quid … so I hope you will be a little more forgiving and lenient than the last lot were.

But I would genuinely like to thank Darren … for agreeing to be my groom today. And thank you, Laura, for allowing Darren to agree. Firstly, on behalf of the bridesmaids, I would like to thank Darren for those kind words. I'm sure you'll agree that you'll remember his wise and witty remarks for the rest of your life … if you have a phenomenal memory … or have nothing else to think about … or meet with a fatal accident on your way home.

So what can I tell you all about a man who came from a humble background and is now rapidly rising to the top of his profession through sheer persistence, grit and willpower. A man of insight, humour and intelligence? A man who is beginning to distinguish himself in his cut-throat commercial world as a winner. Well, that's enough about the best man … I'm here to talk about Darren.

I first met him when he was playing for our arch rivals in the local golf league. I teed off … then he took a swing at his ball and missed it by a mile. He tried again and again and each time he missed it. League game or not, I was getting embarrassed … he wasn't. Finally, he turned to me and said, 'It's a good thing I discovered this early in the game … this course is at least two inches lower than the one I usually play on.'

From that day we became good mates and eventually decided to share a flat together … steady. He's a great lad … with a passion in life … booze. Mind you, it only takes him one drink to get drunk … the fourteenth.

Another thing … as you all know, Darren can be a bit of a fibber … got to be, I suppose … working in banking. Anyway, how well I remember that fateful evening last summer when he came back to our flat and announced he'd met Laura. What he actually said was, 'Neil, you can have my watch … let's hope it works as well for you'… Let me explain …

As we all know, Darren is not lacking in the confidence stakes. That evening he'd called into a pub after work and he saw Laura, sitting at the bar. He eyed her slowly from head to toe and then casually glanced at his watch … *this* watch. 'What's up? Have you been stood up?' she enquired. 'No.' he replied, 'I bought this state-of-the-art watch, and I was just testing it.' Intrigued at this, Laura said, 'A state-of-the-art watch? What's so special about it?' 'It uses gamma rays to telepathically talk to me,' he explained. 'So what's it telling you now then?' 'It's telling me you're not wearing a bra.' Laura giggled and replied, 'Well it must be broken then, because I certainly am.' Darren glared at his watch and said, 'Damn thing must be running an hour fast.'

In all honesty though, it's been a real joy and an absolute privilege being Darren's best man. Perhaps my main duty, other than making this little speech, was to organise the stag weekend. I think we all enjoyed it, didn't we lads? Now Darren's a pretty classy kind of guy, so I thought the stag do should take place somewhere appropriate. I thought about Darren's career in banking, and considered one of the financial capitals of the world ... like Tokyo, New York or Frankfurt. Then I thought about his good looks and superb dress sense and thought perhaps a city renowned for its style, like Paris, Rome or Milan. In the end, I realised there was a town right here in the UK that reflects Darren's personality perfectly ... so we went to West Hartlepool ... now I'm not telling you any tales out of school ... stags' honour and all that ... other than to say he's small ... but perfectly formed ... well it was a bitterly cold night.

Hasn't it been a fantastic day? ... and so emotional ... even this cake's in tiers ... no wedding speech would be complete without that one. And what a wonderful place to hold this do. This place is so posh, you don't ask for the Bill ... you ask for the William. I thought James was thinking of taking early retirement ... God, you'll have to work until you're 500 now to pay for this lot. But honestly, we're all so grateful to you.

Laura, you look absolutely stunning. Married life seems to be suiting you ... When Darren first introduced us, my first reaction was that you were perfect for each other ... and I'm absolutely delighted that you've tied the knot.

Now, as tradition demands, I shall pass on a couple of pearls – or rather trinkets – of wisdom to you both. Actually, it seems a little odd me offering you advice as I'm not married myself. But I'm not worried about that. You know, I could marry anyone I please ... problem is ... I can't seem to please anyone ... but back to my invaluable advice ...

Laura, always remember: if a man buys you flowers for no reason … there's a reason.

Darren, always remember: the secret of a long and happy marriage is to allow time to go out to your favourite restaurant twice a week. A little candlelight, dinner, soft music and dancing … I suggest you go on Tuesdays and Laura goes on Fridays.

Before I draw this to a close, it's time for me to read you a few messages from people who couldn't get here today …

[*Read the genuine messages*]

And finally …

'Dear Laura and Darren, congratulations on your marriage. I trust that your purchases did the trick. Please can you come into the shop and settle your remaining bill as your credit limit has now been reached. Lots of love for the future. Don't be strangers, signed Ann Summers'…. Who is *she*?

[*Look at – and listen to – your watch*] Anyway Darren's old watch is telling me it's time to wind things up … apparently there's a bridesmaid waiting for me … where? … thanks … at the bar …

To end on a serious note … I'd just like to say marriage is not about finding someone you can live with … it's about finding someone you can't live without. I know Darren and Laura well and I know they simply cannot live without each other. And it has to be said that Laura and Darren complement each other in so many ways … the perfect match ... she's hard-working, highly motivated, ambitious, dedicated ... and loves a challenge ... he's that challenge. Let's face it, Darren's no Einstein ... and Laura's always on a diet ... and that's why they are sure to stick together ...through thick and thin.

Let's all drink a toast to them ... to Laura and Darren.

SAMPLE SPEECH 6

Ladies and Gentlemen, Boys and Girls, the last time I made a wedding speech a man fell asleep. I asked a pageboy to wake him, and do you know what the little so-and-so replied? He said, 'You wake him. You were the one who put him to sleep.'

Hi, my name's Neil, and I will do my best not to make the same mistake here today. Mind you, I can't promise *I* won't nod off … I'm knackered. I need my eight hours' sleep and I haven't been getting them recently. I hardly slept a wink at work last week preparing this speech. To be honest, writing it was a nightmare. Where to begin? What to say? Most importantly, what to leave out? Now there are some stories you can tell at a wedding and then there are others that might be interesting to tell, but can't really be told. The ones that Darren invented about himself for the Readers' Letters section of *Men Only* magazine would be perfect examples.

I've known Darren for 10 years now, although my liver claims it's 50 … and my wallet swears it's 100. We've had more good times than I can remember … nothing of course to do with the vast quantities of alcohol we end up drinking. But all that is going to change … or so Laura thinks. Last week I heard Darren tell her he wasn't going to drink any more. Then he turned quietly to me and whispered in my ear: 'But I'm not going to drink any *less* either.'

Now, following tradition, I'm supposed to thank Darren for his kind words, on behalf of the bridesmaids. Crazy, really, because, as you can see, I'm not a bridesmaid. But I'm delighted to do so anyway. Cheers, mate. I know the bridesmaids, ushers and I are all delighted to have played our small part in your big day. And thank you for the kind words you spoke about me ... I don't deserve them ... but I have a bad back and I don't deserve that either.

I'd also like to take this opportunity to say a word or two about this bright and beautiful bride. Yes, Laura has inherited both intelligence and looks from her parents ... I'll leave you to decide which trait comes from Steve and which from Sandra. But I do want to say, in all sincerity: Laura, as Darren has so eloquently explained, I know that today you have made a great friend of mine the happiest man alive.

Well it is with great pride that I stand before you, charged with embarrassing Darren. Throughout the time I have known him, Darren has gone through many life changes to end up the man you see here today. But before we attempt to analyse exactly what went wrong, let's rewind to the early years. Jenny tells me Darren was not the easiest of kids to bring up ... always climbing all over her and never giving her a moment's peace ... that's why she found the playpen so useful ... she sat inside it so he couldn't get near to her.

Then came school ... he was late on the very first day ... fell over and sprained his ankle ... what a lame excuse. Bright lad though ... he asked his teacher what punishment she would give to someone who hadn't done anything. When she said, 'No punishment,' he said, 'That's good ... because I haven't done my homework.' The years flew by and then, one September morning, the neighbours celebrated as Darren went off to uni ... where he met Laura.

Laura was taking Economics and Darren was studying Geography, or, as it was known back then, Beer Drinking. Like most mothers, Sandra had been rather concerned when Laura went off to college for the first time and warned her over and over again never to take any boys back to her room, as it would worry her. At the end of the Christmas term, when Laura went home, she announced to her mother she had met Darren. 'Well I hope you haven't taken him back to your room, Darling. You know that I'd worry about you.' 'No, mum,' she replied, 'I always go back to his room … let *his* mother do the worrying.'

Well things moved on very nicely from there … perhaps a little more quickly than Darren had anticipated. A few months later, during a romantic dinner at the Bengal Spice, Darren knelt down to pick up a piece of chapatti he'd dropped … Laura jumped to conclusions and … well here we all are today.

After college, our hero entered the world of work … or rather was dragged into it kicking and screaming … his first job was on a building site. When he was interviewed for the job, his supervisor asked him if he could make tea. Darren said, 'Yes.' 'And can you drive a forklift truck?' his boss continued. 'Why?' asked Darren, 'How big is the teapot?' He didn't last long there though and moved on … eventually becoming a Contracts Officer.

It's a responsible job and the postholder needs to be 100% trustworthy. Now Darren would never accept a bribe. One day he was offered a Porsche. He was indignant. 'I cannot accept a gift like that,' he fumed. 'I quite understand,' replied the would-be briber, 'I tell you what, why don't I sell it to you for a fiver?' Darren thought about it for a minute and then said, 'In that case, I'll take two.'

Now I'm not suggesting he's a bit iffy, but when we were playing cards last Saturday, Darren suddenly jumped up from the table, white with rage, and yelled, 'Stop the game, Dave's cheating!' How do you know?' I asked. And Darren replied, 'Because he's not playing the hand I dealt him.'

You know, I've learnt so much from this man over the years ... whether we are talking honesty, fashion ... or even haircuts. I've learnt that if I do the exact opposite of what Darren is doing, I won't be going far wrong.

Now, in best wedding speech tradition, I shall offer some not-so-profound advice to you newly-weds ...

Laura, remember that men are like tiled floors ... if you lay them right the first time, you can walk over them for years.

Darren, just remember it only takes a couple of words mumbled in church and you're married ... but it only takes a couple of words mumbled in your sleep and you're divorced.

On that cautionary note, I shall now read the e-mails, texts, cards and other messages we've received from friends and family who couldn't be here to celebrate this magnificent day with us. No doubt, they will be raising a glass to you anyway.

[*Read the genuine messages*]

Okay, this is the last one and it comes from Great Aunty Florence from Florida:

'Sorry I can't be at the wedding, but please send me a photo of the happy couple ... mounted.' Whatever turns you on, Flo ...

One final thought ... it has been said that love is born with the pleasure of looking at each other ... it is fed with the necessity of seeing each other ... it is concluded with the impossibility of separation. You two are inseparable. On behalf of the bridesmaids, I wish you love, health and eternal happiness. Ladies and Gentlemen, I give you the bride and groom.

SAMPLE SPEECH 7

Good afternoon, Ladies and Gentlemen. My name is Neil and I'm about to give Darren the worst few minutes of his life ... which is only fair because Laura's worst few minutes are likely to come later on tonight. But before the fun begins, let me thank Darren for his generous words on behalf of all us attendants ... I've never heard you talk so long or so passionately before about anything that didn't involve tennis.

How I agree that the bridesmaids look absolutely smashing ... and are rightly only outshone by our bride, Laura. I'm sure you'll agree with me, gentlemen, today is a sad day for single men, as another beauty leaves the 'Available' list. And ladies, I'm sure you'll agree with me that ... well, today's passing by without much of a ripple.

You know, I've taken my duties as best man very seriously ... firstly to ensure the groom arrived on time, secondly to ensure the groom arrived sober and thirdly to ensure the groom arrived looking good ... Well two out of three ain't bad ... after all, I'm not a plastic surgeon or a miracle worker. Last week a girl stopped him in the street and said, 'Hi, you gorgeous handsome hunk ... could you show me the way to Specsavers?' But it has to be said: Laura does find him very attractive. Then again, she is on heavy medication. Another important duty – no it's a privilege – is, on behalf of the bridesmaids, to thank Darren for his kind words. I'm sure you'll all agree with Darren and me that they did their job brilliantly.

Isn't it fantastic that Father Brown could join us here this afternoon? Are you enjoying that Irish Cocktail? ... For the uninitiated, an Irish Cocktail is a pint of Guinness with a potato in it. It's funny but there was a priest present at the last reception I attended as well ... and there was a minister there too. When they brought the drinks around, the minister said, 'I'll have a large whisky', whereas the priest said, 'No alcohol for me, I'd rather have a scarlet woman.' At this, the minister put his drink back and said, 'Sorry, I didn't know there was a choice.' Now I don't want to offend anyone present today, so apologies to Father Brown ... and if there is a minister present, apologises to you, too ... but if there is a scarlet woman here ... I'll meet you later behind the bike sheds.

Now what can I say about our blushing bride ... Laura ... you look a million dollars ... sorry, I mean 829,416 euros ... You met Darren during his Bart Simpson years and we all have so much admiration for the way you have dealt with most of his weaknesses ... and that can't have been easy as he has more flaws than the Empire State Building. You are a beautiful lady ... and an even more gorgeous bride. I hope Darren knows what a lucky lad he is. But I still don't know how he ever got her to say 'Yes,' because all she seems to say now is, 'No, Darren, no ... '

Mind you, Laura is right ... Darren does need a kick up the backside every now and then ... For him, work is a four-letter word ... When he graduated from uni, he applied for a job in the Civil Service. At his selection interview he was asked, 'What do you do well?' Darren thought for a moment and then replied, 'Nothing.' 'Good!' cried the selection panel in unison, 'you're just the sort of chap we want ... and we won't even have to break you in.' He tells me he turned up for work on time once ... but there was no one there to appreciate it, so he hasn't bothered since.

But to be fair, Darren is a man of hidden talents ... I just hope that one day he finds them. His main interests away from the office are cookery and tennis. I have heard him described as a cross between Jamie Oliver and Roger Federer ... problem is: he shares Jamie Oliver's tennis skills with Roger Federer's culinary abilities. Last week, Laura asked him if she could have some undercooked chips, some gooey, cold beans and a fried egg coated in old grease. 'Of course not, Babes ... I couldn't possibly give you anything like that,' he said. 'Why not?', she replied, 'That's what you gave me yesterday.'

But, in all honesty, Darren, you are the best mate anyone could ask for ... you have always been there for me when I needed it ... nothing is ever too much for you. That's why I'm so delighted you met, fell in love with ... and have now married Laura. And Laura, believe me, you've found a good man there ... just keep him on his toes ... he has a positive attitude to work ... he is positive he doesn't want to do any ... he's so lazy, he puts bread down the toilet to feed the gulls at the seaside ... don't let him get away with it ...

Now I don't have much advice for the newly-weds, because I really have no experience to speak from. But, having asked some married people earlier for their thoughts, I have come up with the following ...

Darren, keep the toilet seat down ... never argue before you go to bed ... and always say 'Yes, dear' ... unless the question is, 'Does my bum look big in this?'

Laura, if you think the way to a man's heart is through his stomach ... you're aiming too high.

Okay, it's time to read some messages we've received from people who couldn't be here with us in person today …

[*Read the genuine messages*]

These are the last two:

To Laura, We could have been so good together, Robbie Williams

To Darren, We could have been so good together, Robbie Williams

In all seriousness though, this wonderful day would not have been possible without the presence of the two most important people in this room. I think we should raise our glasses to them, don't you? Ladies and Gentlemen, a toast … The bar staff.

No, no … let's drink to two even more important people, the bride and groom. I couldn't be happier for you both. Darren, you are a lucky man. You've found yourself a wonderful wife. Laura, I hope Darren brings you as much happiness as a husband as he's brought to me as a friend. Ladies and Gentlemen, please be upstanding and join me in a toast to two of the nicest people I know … to Laura and Darren.

SAMPLE SPEECH 8

Someone once said being asked to be the best man is like being asked to sleep with the Queen ... it's a great honour to be asked, but nobody really wants to do it. Anyway the Queen is at Balmoral today, so here I am. Well they've done it ... they've finally tied the knot. They've married for better or worse, which is quite appropriate because Darren couldn't have done any better ... and Laura couldn't have done any worse.

Good afternoon, family, friends, fellow guests and any randoms who may have come in out of the rain. ... but weren't we lucky the weather relented just in time for the wedding photos? I'm Neil and for the next few minutes I'm going to be Darren's worst nightmare ... but in a kind, loving and meaningful way, of course.

Firstly though, on behalf of all the attendants, I would like to thank Darren for his kind words and generous gifts. Darren, you are a very fortunate young man ... you've married Laura, who is witty, intelligent and caring. She deserves a good husband. So thank your lucky stars you married her before she found one.

But come on ... I'm sure we'll all agree ... all those hours spent in the beauty parlour getting the hair, make-up and nails just right have really paid off ... Darren, you look beautiful. No, seriously, Laura looks absolutely radiant and the bridesmaids look beautiful too ... Darren, looks ... well, like Darren. That's the compliments bit over, mate ... it's all downhill for you from here.

For those of you who don't know already, I'm Darren's cousin and it is, of course, a great honour to be chosen as his best man. It has been a real pleasure to fulfil this role, but the moment he asked me to do the business for him, it was clear that the most challenging part of the day would be this speech … it wasn't that I hadn't enough to say … far from it … it was having to select only some from the wealth of embarrassing stories which I could have come up with.

Believe me, if I were to regale you with all his embarrassing moments, I would be interrupting myself halfway through to congratulate the happy couple on celebrating their first anniversary … and Uncle Jim over there would be popping out to collect his free bus pass.

Ten minutes ago, Darren implored me not to mention the sheep incident or the reason he has a bicycle repair kit but no bicycle … and I will respect his wishes. But Darren, is it true that if you take sheep to the edge of a cliff, they push back better? … and is it true you only wear button fly jeans because zips scare them off? He also said, 'Why don't you just restrict yourself to talking about the good things about me?' I'll tell you why, Darren: a ten-second speech would be ridiculous.

You know, I've taken my responsibilities as best man very seriously. I think all has gone well so far getting Darren ready for his big day. I got him into a taxi home not on the overnight Eurostar to Paris as a few of his other so-called mates had suggested. He went to bed nice and early and he slept like a baby … he wet the bed three times and woke up crying for his mummy. The condemned man ate a hearty breakfast, dressed immaculately and arrived at the church sober and on time. My one disappointment is my failure to arrange his last request as a single man. I'm so sorry, Darren, but please don't blame me ... there were too many protests from those do-gooders at the Sheep Welfare Council.

For those of you not in the know ... Darren met the lovely Laura at the King's Head ... she was a barmaid and he was their best customer ... he spent so much time there, they charged him rent ... and the staff used to call him Onions because he got pickled so often. When I first met him I thought he was a good health fanatic ... 20 times a day he'd say, 'Good health!'

Anyway, romance seemed to blossom at an alarming rate ... and within weeks they were having proper rows ... A word of advice to you both on that one: Never go to bed mad ... stay up and fight ... then go to bed and make up. But, in all seriousness, I'm absolutely delighted for you both ... you were meant to be.

At this stage it is traditional for a best man to offer some words of advice to the happy couple as they begin a new chapter of their lives. So here goes ...

I had a little chat with Laura about marriage and how her life is going to change. I spoke about the hours of ironing, washing up, babysitting and cooking ... and, Darren, I am delighted to tell you that for the first couple of months Laura has agreed to help you out.

Now Darren ...

It is important to find a woman who cooks and cleans ...

It is important to find a woman who makes good money …

It is important to find a woman who likes to have sex …

And finally, it is important that these three women never meet.

Before we close, it's time for me to read some messages from people who couldn't be here today …

[*Read the genuine messages*]

Oh, that's nice … even the caterers have sent you a message … it says:

'May your honeymoon be like a good Sunday roast: a bit of leg … a bit of breast … and lots of stuffing.'

Now before I wind up, I'd just like to say that over the years Darren has been generous, funny, helpful and, all in all, one of the best mates anyone could ask for … not only to me but to many others of you in the room as well. So, once again, thanks, Darren, for bestowing the honour of being best man upon me. I know you had a choice of many and somehow you managed to whittle down to three … and as I was the only one of them who could read and write, I got the final nod.

In all honesty though, I'm not the best man here today … Darren, you are … and you've just married the best woman … and, I'm sure you'll all agree, together they make the best couple. Ladies and Gentlemen, please be upstanding and join me in a toast to the two of them … to Laura and Darren.

SAMPLE SPEECH 9

NEIL: Good afternoon, Ladies and Gentlemen. My name is Neil and I'm one of Darren's best men. This is Scott, my partner in crime here today.

SCOTT: Hi ... yes, Darren wanted a best man but couldn't find one, so he's got two slightly good ones instead ...

NEIL: No, it was Laura's idea that we do this together ... she reckoned it would take two of us to get him spruced up and to the church on time ...

SCOTT: Well, it certainly took both of us to drag him from the bar last night.

NEIL: But we think we're much more than mere heavies, we're artistes ...

SCOTT: And we'll probably prove that to you later when the booze really starts flowing.

NEIL: Another reason why there are two of us up here today is Darren's indecisiveness ... he just couldn't make his mind up on which of us to ask ...

SCOTT: I know ... I once asked him if he had problems making decisions. He said, 'I'm not really sure about that one.'

NEIL: Well, before we get started, it's my pleasure, on behalf of the bridesmaids, to thank our groom for his kind words and gifts ...

SCOTT: And it's my privilege to thank everyone else involved in making today so special ...

NEIL: Yes, thanks to the ushers for turning up ... I suppose it was too much to have expected them to be sober ...

SCOTT: Come on, be fair. We told them they mustn't look any better than us today ... and they've accomplished that admirably.

NEIL: And doesn't Laura look stunning?

SCOTT: Sure does ... and doesn't Darren look stunned?

NEIL: And a special thanks must go to our generous hosts ...

SCOTT: Generous? That's an understatement ... they may have lost a daughter today ... but they've gained an overdraft.

NEIL: I know, I asked my dad how much it costs to get married. He said, 'I don't know, son, I haven't finished paying yet.'

SCOTT: I don't believe a word of that ... you're close to an idiot.

NEIL: Alright ... I'll move.

SCOTT: Stay there ... we haven't finished yet. You know, when Darren was born, they fired a 21-gun salute ...

NEIL: Pity they missed.

SCOTT: That's not nice ... Did you know Laura calls Darren 'Dog'?

NEIL: Why?

SCOTT: Just a pet name.

NEIL: Wasn't it a lovely buffET lunch today?

SCOTT: Buff*et* ... buff*et* ... the 'T' is silent.

NEIL: Not the way you drink it.

SCOTT: Very funny … How do you manage to say so many stupid
          things in one day?

NEIL: I get up early.

SCOTT: Which is more than Darren does … he's a late riser … until
          this morning he didn't realise there were two eight o'clocks
          in the same day.

NEIL: Do you know what Laura said to him at the end of their first
          date?

SCOTT: No.

NEIL: That's right.

SCOTT: I went out on a date with twins last week.

NEIL: Did you have a good time?

SCOTT: Yes and no.

NEIL: We're not interested in your love life … Darren tells me that
          every time he's finished a meal he has an uncontrollable
          urge to make love on the table.

SCOTT: That's not so strange.

NEIL: Oh, no? Try explaining that to the manager at McDonalds.

SCOTT: Come on, Neil, we're supposed to pass on some words of
          wisdom to Darren now. Any ideas?

NEIL: Well, at bedtime prepare two aspirins and a glass of water
          for Laura. When she says, 'What's that for?' you say, 'For

your headache, dear.' She'll tell you she hasn't got a headache. Then you say, 'Great, then tonight's the night.'

SCOTT: Good advice, mate. Laura's a lovely girl, but the smallest things can upset her ...

NEIL: Not much hope for Darren then ...

SCOTT: No, I didn't mean that ... the other day she was doing a crossword puzzle and she asked Darren, 'What's a female sheep?' He said, 'Ewe,' and she burst into tears.

NEIL: That's not funny ... and Darren asked us not to talk about sheep ...

SCOTT: Oh, yes ... The poor guy's losing his hair, you know. Went to the doctor last week and asked if he could give him something to keep it in.

NEIL: And did he?

SCOTT: Yes, a box.

NEIL: He told me earlier he's really annoyed with himself because he spent half an hour blow-drying his hair this morning ... and then he forgot to bring it with him.

SCOTT: That's not nice ... Darren, great news, mate ... there's a fantastic new treatment for baldness on the market ... it doesn't make your hair grow ... it shrinks your bleeding head to fit what hair you've got left.

NEIL: Now then ... watch your language.

SCOTT: Eh?

NEIL: Watch your language.

SCOTT: English ... what's yours?

NEIL: Do you know what Laura said to Darren at the end of their second date?

SCOTT: Oh, don't be a silly boy ... we've done that one before.

NEIL: That's right.

SCOTT: But enough of this rubbish ... I need a drink.

NEIL: So do I ... let's cut to the telegrams ...

SCOTT: Good idea. Well, before we propose our toast, we'll read some messages from people who couldn't make it here today.

[*Take it in turns to read the genuine messages*]

NEIL: And here are the final two:

SCOTT: To Darren, We could have been so good together, Britney Spears.

NEIL: To Laura, We *were* so good together, Brad Pitt.

SCOTT: Who said good old-fashioned cross-talk comedy was dead?

NEIL: Just about everyone in the room, after hearing us, Scott.

SCOTT: Guess so ... we certainly won't be giving up our day jobs ...

NEIL: True ... but we are genuinely delighted for you both ...

SCOTT: Yes, you are two of our best mates and it's fantastic that you have decided to tie the knot.

NEIL: Ladies and Gentlemen, please stand, raise your glasses, and join us in a toast …

SCOTT: Let us toast the health of the bride …

NEIL: Let us toast the health of the groom …

SCOTT: Let us toast friends far and wide …

NEIL: Let us toast every guest in this room.

SCOTT: We sincerely wish you both every happiness for the future …

NEIL: Ladies and Gentlemen, a toast …

SCOTT and NEIL: The bride and groom.

SAMPLE SPEECH 10

Good afternoon, Ladies and Gentlemen, Boys and Girls. For those of you who don't know me, my name is Julie and I'm Darren's best man. Now I appreciate that it's a little unusual for a girl to be the best man but, according to Laura, none of Darren's male friends could be trusted not to swear, tell dirty jokes, fart or relate the remarkable story of Darren and the Sheepshank ... I think it's something to do with a female in a white fleecy coat ... but you'd better ask him about that yourselves later.

Personally, I think the explanation is far more straightforward ... I make him look taller in the wedding pictures ... he's the only guy I know whose feet can be seen on his passport photo. Choosing me also shows Darren has carefully thought ahead about married life and is happy with women having the last word. Anyway, best man or not, there was no way I was going to put my name down for gender reassignment surgery ... and I'm certainly not going to try to get off with one of the bridesmaids. No offence, girls, you do look fantastic and you've done a marvellous job ... but you have to draw the line somewhere. Anyway, on their behalf, I'd like to thank Darren for his kind and generous words about them.

Now when I was first asked to fulfil this role, I thought: What does a best man do? Reasonable question, you might think. So I did a bit of research and discovered that years ago a best man's job was simply to protect the groom from the bride's family ... Basically, the groom kidnapped the bride and made his escape before her family could do anything about it ... gives a whole new meaning to the phrase 'the dashing best man', doesn't it? Well I reckon Darren is small enough, sorry, I mean big enough to protect himself against

Paul and Lucy.... but if you need any support in a wedding day tag wrestling bout, I'm your girl … but please watch the hairdo.

But seriously, it's great to see Laura and Darren getting it together today … as it were. Today Laura's the confident, woman-about-town you see before you … but a few years ago she wasn't at all like that. Laura and me have been best mates since school … it was a wonderful time of dodgy hairdos, zits and constant arguments over whether to listen to the Spice Girls or Boyzone … and when we got together it was like Catherine Tate meets Little Britain … We got up to allsorts but would never admit to it or back down on anything … Laura was a bit like Vicky Pollard … in attitude … not looks … 'Yeah but, no but, yeah but, no but … Shut up, I haven't done anything' … and I was stroppy Lauren … 'Am I bovvered?' … No I wasn't …

Anyway, somehow we got through those awkward years and then Laura met Darren at … Glastonbury 2004 … I always admired what these two had when they were dating. They used to travel for hours to meet each other on weekends. I wonder how they'll fill free time since they won't be travelling any more? Oh, yeah, they're newly-weds and I'm sure they'll find *something* to do …

Darren's a great lad … he has so many wonderful qualities … brains, charm, looks … are just a few of the ones he's missing. Mention *soixante-neuf* to him and he thinks you're trying to sell him 60 eggs … This man is so unlucky that if he went into the funeral business people would stop dying … I think what Laura likes about him most is that he's utterly unspoilt by failure.

No, you two are great people and I'm proud to count myself as one of your friends. Without wishing to get all soppy, I'd really like to say how much I love you both ... in a platonic sort of way of course, Darren ... before you get any ideas ... and I wish you both the very best for your future together ... you both deserve it.

Now how can Laura and Darren ensure a happy marriage? I know they've already had loads of advice that has been handed down from generation to generation ... and been ignored by most of them. That's because most of this advice is given by men ... and to men. What do they know? Well, I'm a woman and I can tell you like it really is. It's all about communication. Darren, here's a quick lesson on female speak which you would be wise to reflect upon ...

When Laura uses the word 'Nothing', she actually means 'something' ... you know: 'What's wrong, love?' ... 'Oh, nothing',

... and when she says, 'Go ahead', this means, 'Do it if you want ... I don't really want you to ... but I've lost interest',

... and when she says, 'Fine', this really means, 'Look, I'm right ... and your best bet is to shut up.'

So Darren, if you hear Laura say 'nothing', 'go ahead' and 'fine' within a couple of minutes of each other, be on your guard ... but remember you, too, have a few words to fall back on ... 'yes' ... 'dear' ... 'buy it'.

I hope that clears up any misunderstandings ...

Turning to Laura … I offer this piece of advice …

If you love something, set it free,
If it comes back, it was, and always will be yours.
If it never returns it was never yours to start with.
And, if all it does is just sit in your house, mess up your stuff, spend your money, eat your food and drink too much … then you'd be married to Darren.

Well, we've all had a fantastic time, but unfortunately some people couldn't be here in person to share your special day. Don't worry … they haven't forgotten you. Here are a few messages they've sent …

[*Read the genuine messages*]

I don't know who these last people are. Do you know a Bob and Alice, Darren? Anyway, I'll read their message to you:

'Congratulations on your wedding. Hope you are having a wonderful day. From Bob Farkin, Alice Farkin … and the whole Farkin family.'

And now the toast … Wise are they who sense that the surest way to be fully loved is to love fully. Let us raise a glass to two wise people as they form their new life together … Sorry, you say you haven't got any champers left in your glass? … Am I bovvered? … Am I bovvered? … Ladies and Gentlemen: I give you the bride and groom.

A FINAL WORD

Well all good things must come to an end ... and so must this book. I hope you found it useful and amusing ('What page was the joke on?' I hear you ask.)

Problem is ... I just can't win. If everything goes brilliantly, you're not going to say you got it all from a book, are you? No way. You're going take all the credit yourself. But if you lose the ring and make the speech from Hell, you'll blame it all on me and post a crappy review on Amazon.com.

Anyway, it's been fun talking to you. Have a nice (wedding) day. Missing you already.

Resources

BOOKS
You are reading the only book you really need. However, if, like Oliver, you want more, here are some suggestions …

Best man's duties
The Best Best Man, Jacqueline Eames (Foulsham)
The Best Man's Organiser, Christopher Hobson (Foulsham)

While both have something to offer, they are a little dated. A more modern interpretation of your role can be found in:

The Best Man's Wedding, Confetti.co.uk (Octopus Publishing Group)

Speaking in public
For me, by far the best book on speaking in public is:

Just Say a Few Words, Bob Monkhouse (Virgin Books). Bob was special.
   Other useful offerings from mere mortals include:

Handbook for the Terrified Speaker, Mitch Murray (Foulsham)
Speaking in Public, John Bowden (Essentials)

Best man's speech
Each of the following contains sample lines and sample speeches. Please don't simply crib them. Remember that your speech should be original, relevant and personal.

Be the Best Best Man …, Philip Khan-Panni (How To Books)
Making the Best Man's Speech, John Bowden (How To Books)
The Best Man's Speech, Confetti.co.uk (Octopus Publishing Group)
Best Man Best Speech, Dominic Bliss (New Holland)

Wedding speeches

The same advice applies when referring to these more general
wedding speech titles:

One-liners for Speeches and Special Occasions, Mitch Miller (Foulsham)
One-liners for Weddings, Mitch Miller (Foulsham)
Your Brilliant Wedding Speech, Helen Smith (Foulsham)
Speeches, Confetti. co.uk (Octopus Publishing Group)
Making a Great Wedding Speech, Philip Calvert (How To Books)
Making a Wedding Speech, John Bowden (How To Books)

Stag dos

Stuck for stag do ideas? Then this is the book for you:

The Alternative Stag, Genna Hayman and Kirstie Rowson (Virgin Books)

WEBSITES

There are thousands – maybe millions – of wedding and stag-related
websites out there. If you can't afford to go surfing in Hawaii, at least
you can spend some quality time surfing the net. The following is
intended as no more than a brief review of some of the huge range
of possibilities. The inclusion of a particular site does not imply
recommendation. Ultimately, it's down to you and the happy couple
to select the most suitable one(s), given your specific requirements.

Weddings and receptions

General
Here are just a handful of wedding and reception sites:

www.2-in-2-1.com
www.confetti.co.uk
www.hitched.co.uk
www.ourmarriage.com
www.weddingbells.com
www.weddings-and-brides.co.uk
www.weddingchannel.com
www.weddingguide.co.uk

Church weddings
To find all the requirements and procedures for getting married in church, see:

www.findachurch.co.uk

Civil ceremonies
If it's going to be a civil ceremony, the most informative website is:

www.www.registerofficeweddings.com

Civil partnerships
The Civil Partnership Act 2004 came into force in December 2005. This enables same sex couples to obtain legal recognition of their relationship. Although, legally speaking, they are not 'weddings' as such, civil partnership ceremonies pretty much follow the conventions of a civil wedding ... and that includes having one or more best men and/or best girls. For more details, log on to:

www.civilpartnerships.org.uk

www.stonewall.org.uk

Specific faiths and cultures

In our multicultural society, interfaith marriages are becoming more
and more common. A good general site which includes discussion
on related issues is:

www.interfaithmarriage.co.uk

If you want/need to find out more about the beliefs and traditions of
a specific faith and culture, log on to the relevant site:

Hindu

www.lalwani.demon.co.uk/sonney/wedding.htm

Humanist

www.humanism.org.uk/weddings

Jewish

www.beingiewish.com/cycle/wedding.html

Mormon

www.templemarriage.com

Muslim

www.mybindi.com/weddings/ceremonies/muslim/cfm

Sikh

www.sikhs.org/wedding

Limousine hire

Obviously, it will be preferable to choose a company based reasonably close to you. So include the name of your biggest local town/city in any search. Here is a sample of some providers throughout the UK:

www.american-limousines.co.uk (Organised by UK postcode)
www.stretched-4-u.co.uk
www.callalimo.co.uk
www.limohiredirectory.com
www.limoshop.co.uk

Wedding car decorations

Okay, it's a cliché, but it simply has to be done …

www.confetti.co.uk.shopping
www.weddingwonderland.net/

Music

The music played at a ceremony and reception can help set just the right tone and atmosphere. Here are a few sites that may be of interest to the bride and groom:

www.pnms.co.uk
www.mfiles.co.uk
www.gig-guide.co.uk
www.hiway.co.uk
www.excite.co.uk

Wedding suit hire

If you are thinking about hiring suits online, here are a few suppliers:

www.wedding-service.co.uk
www.menswear-hire.co.uk
www.countywedding.co.uk

Wedding gifts

Many large retail stores offer an online wedding gift service. Here are a few other specialist suppliers:

www.thegiftexperience.co.uk
www.bust-ed.co.uk
www.shopsafe.co.uk
www.greatgifts.org
www.coolershopping.co.uk

STAG DOS

General

There are hundreds of companies that specialise in organising stag nights and weekends. Here is a sample of them:

www.activepursuits.com
www.brilliantweekends.co.uk
www.chillisauce.co.uk
www.crocodileevents.co.uk
www.eclipseleisure.co.uk
www.fantastic-days.com
www.greatescapes.co.uk
www.lastnightoffreedom.com
www.organize-events.co.uk
www.releasetravel.co.uk
www.stagweb.co.uk
www.stagweekends.co.uk

Accessories/fancy dress/customised T-shirts

Come on, bestie, let's make this a night to remember. Here are some possible sources:

www.hen-stagpartyshop.co.uk

www.custardpie.co.uk

www.directory.justfancydress.co.uk

www.absolutelycharming.co.uk

www.anyspecialoccasion.co.uk

www.chikenshop.co.uk

www.screenprinting.uku.co.uk

www.otlinegroup.co.uk

Strippers

There are loads of sites specialising in the booking of strippers, lap-dancers, stripograms, kissograms, adult comedians and other nocturnal delights. Here are a few of them:

www.lastnightoffreeedom.co.uk

www.ukclassifieds.co.uk

www.fullservice.co.uk

www.stripagram.co.uk

www.kissa-gram.co.uk

Index